Passion
and
Policy

OTHER BOOKS BY ALVIN L. SCHORR

Filial Responsibility in the Modern American Family, 1961

Slums and Social Insecurity, U.S. (1963) and Great Britain (1964)

Social Services and Social Security in France, 1964

Poor Kids, 1966

Explorations in Social Policy, 1968

Children and Decent People (editor), U.S. (1974) and Great Britain (1975)

Jubilee for Our Times (editor), 1977

"Thy Father and Thy Mother," A Second Look at Filial Responsibility and Family Policy, 1980

Common Decency: Domestic Policies After Reagan, 1986

Cleveland Development: A Dissenting View (editor), 1991

The Personal Social Services: An Outside View, Great Britain (1992)

Passion and Policy

A SOCIAL WORKER'S CAREER

Alvin L. Schorr

DAVID PRESS
CLEVELAND, OHIO

Printed in the United States of America
Jacket and text design by Mort Epstein
*Cover photograph of the Poor People's March on Washington in 1968
courtesy of the* Cleveland Press *Archives at Cleveland State University*

Library of Congress Catalog Card Number: 97-68258
ISBN 0-940601-12-5 (Hardcover)
ISBN 0-940601-13-3 (Softcover)

This book

is dedicated to

our young grandchildren,

Talia, Lily and Jeremy,

whom Ann and I love

with all our hearts.

Contents

Introduction

Over the years, my work on government policy led to an increasingly inclusive view of the perspectives from which one should view specified policies—social, humanitarian, administrative, political and financial (i.e., efficiency). At one point I subtitled a professional article "A Cubist Policy Analysis," to emphasize this point of multiple, simultaneous perspectives.[1]

This book is about how one works at developing policy in a Cubist way, specifically how I worked at getting policies implemented and what I learned. As the name of the book may suggest, it is about policy work that is performed out of conviction, not simply as a technician or an *apparatchik*.

Despite this view about multiple perspectives, I rarely thought about the manner in which my own work was shaped by my early circumstances and development. For example, when I was a so-called family life specialist in the Social Security Administration in 1958, out of the broad palette of the agency's programs I chose Aid to Dependent Children as my first subject. I spent an uninterrupted year working on it and a good deal of time, in chunks, thereafter. It was not chosen because I knew much about it; I did not. Yet, it did not enter my mind that a reason for my choice was that my family had received welfare, nor did I refer to the fact in the course of my work until long afterwards.

In 1973, I became general director of the Community Service Society of New York (CSS), a wealthy, prestigious voluntary social service organization. It was in a considerable state of disarray, having wiped out its main activity—family counsel ing—without settling on new activities. (After extended review, the board had concluded that the effectiveness of such work had been made clear and need no longer be demonstrated.) Organizational missions ought to be worked out over a period of time, engaging all the chief actors and using such research as may be available. But at CSS, many staff members had been dismissed and many who remained had no real function. Confusion reigned.

I concluded that we did not have time to stand still and study. After just a month of consultation and reflection,spent reviewing the history and capacities of CSS and surveying the terrain of pain in New York City, I proposed seven new projects for trustee approval. One would demonstrate how to help single parents. Did I reflect that I had been raised in a single-parent family (my father having died when I was two)? Why, no.

Another recollection brings to mind Citizen Kane's "Rosebud." I have a fragmentary memory of standing in my mother's kitchen (perhaps three or four year's old, I was not as tall as the counter) and crying for *gogelmogel*. My mother was frantic; she could not make out what I wanted. I have since learned that in Hungarian or Polish *gogelmogel* is a creamy blend of eggs, milk and other good things. Scraps of conversation when I was young led me to conclude that I had, at least briefly, been in a foster family home—a Hungarian foster home. Doubtless, my foster mother had been trying to fatten me up.

A widow with two children, working a sixty-hour week as a seamstress, my mother may well have concluded that she should arrange that someone else care for her younger son. When away, however, apparently I cried without pause and so she had to take me home and manage somehow. I don't think that I ever asked her about this episode directly, nor would she have said much if I asked. Are *gogelmogel* and *blessaw,* the other word that seems to have come home with me, connected with my perennial preoccupation with children in substitute care? It would be hard to think not.

Even though I was trained as a social caseworker, to whom making such connections becomes habitual, these memories survived in a separate compartment. It was not until I was well advanced in my career that I connected my childhood with my work. It seems to me that this personal dimension, too, is a dimension of a Cubist analysis of social policy. In particular, feelings and convictions may be carried into one's work without critical examination. And such memories, attended to or not, power one's work.

For these reasons, among others no doubt, I set forth here as nearly a candid view of my early development as it is possible for me to have published. It takes shape as a letter to my mother, which is how it came to my mind in the years after she died. Here and there, where the connection seems to me to be direct and clear, I point out the effect of my personal experiences on the way that I worked at social policy. The reader may easily conclude that there are other connections.

This contribution to "psychohistory" continues a small and special thread in social science, especially in psychology. For my taste, however, the social scientists' efforts to order and systematize these biographies tend to leave them stilted.[2]

The "Letter to My Mother" is Chapter 1 of this book. For as long as I remember, our family was three people—my mother, my older brother and myself. My brother, Danny as I have always known him, or Dan Schorr as he is widely known, worked from a young age and was much out of our home. He was nevertheless an important figure to me; I often concluded childhood arguments with "my brother, who is in junior high school!, says . . ." In time, he became a famous television and radio newscaster and commentator.

Chapter 2 describes the times in which I grew up and my years at the City College of New York. It offers a sequential account of my journey through graduate school and the jobs that, by a road no engineer would have laid out, led me to government work: family counselor in St. Louis, psychiatric social worker in New Jersey, supervisor in a public assistance and children's agency in Maryland, director of a demonstration of how to organize a counseling program in a "defense impact" area in Ohio and director of Family Service of Northern Virginia. All this took place between 1943 and 1958. Readers who picked up this book to learn about public policy may find this chapter less interesting and may want to skip it.

Chapters 3 through 7 are also sequential (though with a digression here and there), covering the years from 1958 through 1969 when I worked in government: as a family life specialist and then acting director of long range research at the Social Security Administration (an agency of the U.S. Department of Health, Education and Welfare—HEW); as director of research at the Office of Economic Opportunity (the "Poverty Program"); and then once more at HEW as deputy assistant secretary. In the academic year 1962–63, I was given a leave of absence from the Social Security Administration to take up a Fulbright fellowship at the London School of Economics.

When I left the government in 1969, I had what I privately considered a "decompression grant" from the Ford Foundation, allowing me to teach at Brandeis University and consult with municipal governments about how to use government grants for income maintenance programs. In 1970, I became dean of the New York University School of Social Work and went on in 1973 to be general director of the Community Service Society. My subsequent work as a professor of social work in Cleveland from 1979 on is touched on only incidentally here.

Despite all this change over the years, the themes of my work seemed to be durable: children, the family, poverty and inequality. Mollie Orshansky, who devised the government definition of poverty, would say, astutely and enviously, that I changed jobs often enough but never seemed to change the work I was doing.

Other things were going on at the same time, of course. I was editor of the journal *Social Work*. I spoke and wrote widely in popular and professional venues. I worked on the presidential campaign of U.S. Senator George McGovern. From time to time, I published a book meant to advance a point of view; never a textbook—the idea of writing a textbook bored me. For my money, the most interesting of these books are *Poor Kids, Slums and Social Insecurity* and *Common Decency: Domestic Policies After Reagan.*

Chapter 8 is a reflection on how I came to view the practice of social policy—its relation to the social sciences, lessons learned, the power and limitations of reason. The final chapter, Chapter 9, assesses the current social reality, in many ways a more stressful and difficult reality than my generation faced, and poses choices that may be made.

What follows may be read for a variety of purposes: uncovering the child in the working policy man, using the content for case studies in policy, judging how to advance in policy work or inventing one's own policy role as, in some sense, every policy worker does. Or, one can regard this material as a stand for liberalism—for, certainly, I have been a liberal throughout my career—and judge whether liberalism deserves the bum rap it has lately had.

The reader will see that I set all this forth without apology (though I made mistakes, of course). On the contrary, I recommend the underlying point of view to my grandchildren, to whom this book is dedicated. It has led to a sometimes stormy but rich working life, even when my goals were not achieved.

Several publishers have thought the structure of this book odd, mixing childhood memory, professional memoir and contemporary reflection, and not likely to sell. Though one point of this book is that, in a measure, these are all one, undoubtedly the publishers are right about the market. Consequently, I am more than a little grateful to the Mandel School of Applied Social Sciences of Case Western Reserve University and its dean, Darlyne Bailey, for believing that the book is important and undertaking to have it published.

Many people have helped. My wife, Ann, has read the manuscript with sympathy and honesty and, besides, provided unfailing support when we might have been doing other things that would be satisfying for both of us. My brother, Dan, and my children, Jessica, Kenneth and Wendy, brought their own recollections of our life together and their own expertise to the reading of this material and offered useful comments.

I have turned for reaction and for snippets of information to people who shared experiences with me. Robert A. Levine, Bertram Beck, Gertrude S. Goldberg, Robert W. Sweet, Mitchell Ginsberg, Marcia Stein and Eleanor Korman took time to respond critically and constructively. Herbert Gans and S. M. (Mike) Miller also read chapters and offered solid advice. In the midst of researching her own book about welfare, Blanche D. Coll provided information for mine. Alvin Sallee offered advice, much of which I did not take, but he encouraged me, anyway. I am more grateful than I can say for all this time, judgment and good will.

Every author knows the value of an intelligent and conscientious editor, and I have had one: Diana Tittle. It is a cleaner book, better organized and more intelligible because of her devoted work.

Finally, I thank the Mandel School and Eleanor Gerson for their support of these efforts.

In the end, of course, I alone am responsible for what appears here. Not only did I write it; I lived it.

NOTES

1. Alvin L. Schorr, "The Refundable Tax Credit—A Cubist Policy Analysis," *Policy Analysis,* 18, 1985, pp. 333–55.

2. Edwin G. Boring and Gardner Lindzey, eds., *A History of Psychology in Autobiography,* vol. V, Appleton-Century-Crofts, New York, 1967. Volumes I to III appeared between 1930 and 1936 and volume IV in 1952. A more recent attempt at psychohistory, approached somewhat differently, deals with eight people in economics, political science and sociology. See Bernard Barber, *Effective Social Science,* Russell Sage Foundation, New York, 1987.

Letter
to My Mother

Dear Mother,

I am not sure what it means to address a letter to you, as you have died. But so much went unsaid; its true extent dawned on me only in going through the few papers you kept in all the moves from apartment to apartment. You used to ask that I say Kaddish for you on the anniversary of your death, and I promised. This letter is a secular Kaddish.

I dimly remember the name Arnold Miller from boyhood. But what was he to you that for forty years you kept a carbon copied announcement of the party when he sailed for Europe? If there was to be a memento, why the announcement of his departure? And how is it that I never heard about the man who proposed that you marry him when you were already seventy years old? If I had known and asked, you would have dismissed him as foolish—beneath attention. But apparently you seriously if only briefly considered the idea.

I had thought of you as living somewhat aloof, in touch to be sure with your brothers and sister and friends and neighbors, but not more deeply involved with others than you were with me. Visiting you in the hospital, I was astonished at the number of people who moved through your room—some obviously close and some in your debt. One young woman I invited to lunch and quizzed, trying to grasp the nature of your engagement with someone the age of your grandchildren.

Why should I have been surprised? After all, how much did I tell you about myself? Withholding was the arrangement between us, from the time I was a teenager if not before. But I had others to talk to. Your friends and debtors, were there two or three among them in whom you confided, or were you so proud that you talked intimately to no one?

One of my last memories of you closed a circle to my earliest. I came to see you in the intensive care unit, a cubicle behind a glass wall. Confused, frightened, stubborn, you wanted to go home, and it fell to me to say that was not possible. Poking to the core of the issue, you asked, "You mean that I am not in charge of myself?"—with disbelief, chagrin, despair, as if this were so for the first time in your life. Maybe, despite all the travail, it *was* the first time.

Turning to go, I stubbed my toe on the door, my glance skittered across the glass partition, and my mind went straight back fifty years to the Willard Parker Hospital for Contagious Diseases: a child, alone in a large bed in a large room, in the distance a glass partition and you on the other side—a young woman in a fur-like coat. I dropped a cloth toy on the crisp sheet and reached for it; it had tumbled too far. You turned from the partition in distress. Both the separation and the bond in that turning bind me still.

Isolation for contagious diseases was the practice in those days; perhaps it is still. I had not remembered that hospital scene for years. It shook me that it would light up like that—intact, waiting for the click of a switch.

There was a circle closed for you too in that intensive care unit. It was your conviction, and for a time I thought that you were right, that my father, your husband, died in a building—it now looks like a remnant of Imperial Rome—of the same hospital a year before I came down with polio (or diphtheria or scarlet fever, or whichever illness I was remembering). It was there that you were to die too.

Among your papers were just four letters from my father. He was overcome to the point of tears by his illness, funny about his pretensions, and tender about your responsibilities. But before all that he had been ambitious, "hustling" one might say now, digging for his cache in this gold mine—America. We would have been rich if he had lived. I do not think you remembered him very well. He came across from you as a romantic figure—handsome, delicate, poetic, victimized, good. He made you promise that his sons would go to college. I always resented and defied your inclination to conventional piety—in family matters, in social behavior, in religion. But it was not until I read his letters that I realized how different he probably was from the Keats-like image of him that I had assimilated from you.

There were to be many separations and hospitals for me. A boy of six now, in an adult ward, I was to have an operation to correct the damage polio had done to my foot. Sitting up in bed, I tried uneasily to get my bearings. An orderly started rolls of toilet paper going down the rows of beds. Each patient tore off a length of paper and passed on the roll. It seems impossible, but I didn't understand the transaction and concluded that we would be given scissors and involved in some game to pass the time. When bedpans were brought, I was ashamed to ask for one and, anyway, had kept only two squares of paper. I do not mean to sound pathetic. These were not the stretches of time when I longed for you. This was the ordinary round of my days and tasks—negotiating rapids and shoals in which what people might think of my behavior was always more delicate and painful than the practical problem itself.

It was during the long nights that I thought about you, and the long stretches of days when I was in pain or frightened. (Would they operate? Would the doctor remove the cast? How long would this go on!) I must have invented my own yoga, for I submerged my sense of life process inside, trying to leave pain outside. If I let it all pass over me, I would survive. And if that could be brought off, I would be good—make no demands, no trouble, no noise, no tears—and you would know that I was good and come to visit. Other relatives must have come—uncles and aunts and, in adolescence, friends; if so, I do not remember. My doctor, Dr. Boorstein, came of course. He was your friend and coworker in the Zionist movement, and kind to me. I believed I received favored treatment in the hospital because of him.

Prompted by your death and by other separations of which, of course, you would not have known, I have thought about how I clung to the idea of you. I have found that almost at will I can induce a detached state—in my head a fugue-like sound all its own, like a radio station's transmitting signal, very faint. It is a state of suspension and waiting: You are there. You will come. On that signal, I am encased in timelessness.

Systems of interpretation are like tongues. One can describe the world with reality and reasonably tight logic in French or German, or a language that relies on clicks, or another in which tone conveys meaning. Social interpretations of behavior are not better than psychological, "now" interpretations not better or worse than delving into early childhood. Each adds at least a marginal dimension of meaning. Which is used at any moment may depend on which most powerfully provides meaning and carries emotional conviction.

Understood in this qualified way, it has seemed to me that much of the drive that animates me in later life goes back to those hospitals and enforced stays in bed. I postponed gratification, as my sometimes colleagues would say, and without thinking about it stored up a considerable credit on my gratification account. Avidity and greed are plainer words. The world owed me later what it had not delivered earlier—and a bonus for waiting. I accepted but deeply resented being moved about, made to wait, disposed of by adults talking over my head and behind closed doors. I must have said to myself that a time would come when nothing ever again would arbitrarily be done to me. Even at this distance from the event, anger rises in me as I write the words. And I must have looked from outside at the child I was and taken him and others like him as my lifelong wards. It is a curious fact about social reformers that some are partisans of the aged and some of children. Few develop equally strong feelings about both groups; no one seems to know why. For myself, at any rate, I know.

You wonder what all this is to you, Mother. I will come to it in a moment.

I was talking about hospitalization and separation. Some years afterward, my first real girlfriend undertook to marry someone else. (Though not so wild as to propose marriage, I was besotted with her.) And my complaint rang a note the most painful source of which I didn't yet recognize. In what was meant to be my last letter to her, I wrote that I was left lonely and insular—a common enough sentiment in the circumstance. Yet it was not by any means our last communication. Sporadically, we had something to do with one another over the years until I married. Then there was an angry note from her and it appeared that, for once, I had done the leaving.

Bruno Klopfer, the once widely known psychologist and expert on Rorschach tests, wrote that a solid affair or marriage is a union of complementary neuroses. Some twenty-five years after that second separation, my one-time girlfriend and I met by accident and I proposed a private conversation. She told me then, a little angrily because she was smarting from having agreed to come at my convenience, her neurosis about me. Her father had been married to two women at once—tacitly understood but never mentioned in her family; like him, I had faded in and out of her life. I came and went and came again without explanation. Now I summoned her and, despite all that had intervened, she came without a thought. I had irresistibly mimicked her father but, adult, she would be bound no longer. As for my neurosis, when she had shut the door on me it was against a background of shut doors.

She said a fascinating thing about having married someone else. She had to decide whether it is better in marriage to love more or be loved more. She decided that her husband would be the one who loved more and that was better.* Wanting to be the one who loved less was not my wish, Mother, and would not have been yours. I do not speak of love in particular but of passion. What you felt you felt entire, though you might not voice it. I knew that about you (how was one not to know?), and may have that from you. The passions I mentioned a few paragraphs back—that I was owed more than my share, that I was not to live by unexplained or indefensible rules—ran head-on into your passions, did they not? For you too were owed more than your share. And you lived by rules—most relevantly, the rule of duty that in time you thought I owed you. So our passionately if not bitterly held premises were at odds, and unstated.

A little late, I was ready to enter school and we hoped that I might join my age group in first grade. The principal must have looked at and taken me in, for he said that I was socially not ready for first grade and must go to kindergarten. I recall the first sight of children playing on the floor by twos and threes—activities I understood about as well as I had understood the passing of the bedpans. If first grade seemed better than kindergarten, probably it was only because there would be some real business to which I could address myself instead of these strange children. Against both our wills, I was now set afloat on a current to adulthood. You were upset because I was upset and you could not rescue me. Surely, friends assured you that

---

*W. H. Auden saw this otherwise. The plaque on the building in Greenwich Village where he wrote quotes him as follows:

If equal affection cannot be,
Let the more loving one be me.

kindergarten would be good for me. God only knows what might have been good for me. I must make my way.

It got through to me as an adult that, in addition to all the other duties and cares of a young widow, you had been working ten hours a day, six days a week (here were the roots of my lifelong support for the trade union movement). And I always sick. And the Zionist movement. And helping my grandmother and other family members just over from Europe. I had known all this in some general way, of course, but cannot recall grasping how it must have felt for you. When sick, I simply wanted attention. When well, I felt sometimes neglected, at other times tenderly (anxiously?) close to you, but in neither case focused on *you*, I fear.

Quite early, I spent much of my time on the street with neighborhood kids. Jacks, immies, pitch the penny, teacher may I?, card games—mostly conducted sitting or crouched over in intimate proximity to street and curb—and such softball games as from time to time I could manage. If one of us had and would part with a penny, it might be laid on a track in order to derail the streetcar. My typical state after a day's play was filthy. Aside from being as good as a club jacket in a closed boys' world (your expression of horror was part of the pay-off), I think being dirty meant I was one with the street. My attention went outward to the physical street and group of kids rather than inward to myself or you or other particular people; it was a withdrawal, easy, a relief. It gave us some peace with each other.

(In your last months, after a sleepless night trying to puzzle it out, you would search my face when I came to visit, and ask, "How did I manage to do it all?" The truth is, I could not imagine.)

After some months of psychotherapy as a young man, I achieved a kind of compassion for the difficulties you had faced. My new maturity was marked by switching to address-ing you as "Mother" instead of "Ma" (in two syllables—Ma-ah, rising or falling on the second, depending on whether questioning or peremptory); surely you noticed. But my understanding was merely the superficial, contracted-for-in-advance result of therapy. Underneath were sustained hurt and anger.

I did not really forgive you then, nor did such warmth as I summoned last very long. Neither did you proffer much warmth to me. It was a Versailles Treaty of the emotions I offered—expressions of amity spread over untouched difficulties, and that was not your way, not with me. You had primary requirements of me—that I should marry a Jewish girl, that I should be successful at work, and that I should show you necessary respect. (With some astonishment, I observe that I did all that, don't you think so? About the last you are not so sure.) And you would not mask those requirements or trade your chance of getting them for peace or friendship. As for lesser requirements, having to do with religious observance, my friends, my conduct, my particular kind of work and way of thinking, a steady disapproval marked your acceptance of my choices which were, perforce, your necessity.

If you had an intimate, you told him I was stubborn.

These are hard things I have just said, that you were demanding and not warm, but I believe I have this from you—not flinching from saying hard things if they are true. It is a kind of respect; things are what they are and pretense dishonors.

To be like you in some ways is perhaps the most honor I have done you. I recall the announcement that I would be a social worker. (Those were the days, the end of the 1930s, when a choice of a career was a joke or a prayer. What I was really announcing was that I would spend two more years in college, not itself an offensive idea.) It was not a joke to you—you were appalled: A woman's profession! A snoop in other people's closets! I had gone over to the enemy or out of my mind. In the ensuing chill, I had a sense of wonder that you missed that I was behaving as you would, that is, doing what I must do.

In your last days, you provided your final illustration of autonomy. Your chin, mouth and nose seized up in the respirator's rubber clutch—a bio-mechanical snout out of some mad scientist's fantasy, the machine sucked your chest in and pushed it out. It was a humiliation you would not have borne, if you knew and if you could manage. You would have struck it away scornfully, saying, "Let me go. It is time anyway." Others thought otherwise, but I thought you died because you decided to die.

Other women who have known me well, not to say other people, not to say people I have dealt with in the course of work, have also thought me stubborn. (Tenacity may more exactly convey how this translated into work.) But perhaps you are not pleased that I should entirely credit it to your example.

Uncle Louis, with whom we lived for a while, was I suppose as nearly a father figure as I was to have. It was understood that he was doing us a favor, and he had his own baby daughter—certainly unfair competition for his affection. Still, he was kind in his stern way, and he took time to teach me chess. Then a hush enveloped him and it was understood that he was sick; then, it was cancer. At the end, there was some talk about whether he, an avowed atheist, would see the rabbi. It was said that when the rabbi came to see him as he lay dying, Uncle Louis waved him away and turned his back. There, I thought, was a man! For some time afterward, a Talmudic habit I must have had from uncles, I imagined his conversation with God about this: "As I see you plainly, I must admit the possibility that I was wrong, but surely you would not have approved of last-minute cowardice." And God turns away, muttering something about chutzpah.

Long afterward, I crossed the ocean to see a friend and teacher who also, it was tacitly understood, was dying of cancer. Another protégé had been closer to him, but in time had chosen a more militant road. It had led to a public falling out—a painful matter all around. Now he wished to see him, at least *see* him, and Richard was not willing. I brought the matter up at dinner with Richard: *Friends might differ about policy. They had much longer been very close than at odds. In what way would it hurt to see him? In what way represent a concession in point of view?* He brushed me off. *Dying* (unspoken) *was a cheap and irrelevant reason for coming to terms. He would not, for sentimental reasons, undo the falling out.* History and positions taken were realities. There was an impressive solidity about the positions taken between people; and I thought of you.

Determination, independence, respect for books—these are qualities I may have from you. But when did you love me so I was able to love others, and if not you, then who? For some years, we were surrounded by others, some of them certainly fond. My "bubbe," your mother, I remember as an old woman, of whose strangeness (the dark dress of a peasant widow, her sour odor that I thought of as age, and the fact that she spoke only Yiddish) I was a little afraid. But I stole pennies from her purse and she knew and did not mind. My uncles, my Aunt Ethel were certainly kind, but none seems central.

And there is the mystery of the source of the energy it took to be stubborn. Quite early, life shoved me about: the illnesses and long separations, father dead. The capacity to be stubborn has to be rooted somewhere. Was it before my memory of myself and you, before the entire burden of a livelihood and two young children was thrust upon you, that we formed a bond that I clung to desperately for the next years?

I greatly suspect that with this surmise I have invented a golden age but, if so, we are left with the mystery of what fueled the long struggle and long loves and friendships.

As a boy, I had much dependence on and love for you. My brother quite early became the man in the family—maybe not so sweet for him, all in all, but preempting the evident role in which I might have been close to you. On rare occasions, I brought you small gifts or did small favors but, mostly, I was too awkward or too needful myself. Walking home from school at age eight or so, I explained to another boy that he could not hope to love his mother as much as I: I had spent long, lonely hours in bed; my mother had made great sacrifices for me; it made a strong and unusual bond. I should feel more compassion for the child I was. Now he embarrasses me—his priggishness and defenses so evident, he plainly so vulnerable.

I never learned to wall myself off, Mother. If I had become cool and remote to defend myself, I might have been more comfortable but in later years would have lost much of the capacity for intimacy. So I was vulnerable to you all your life, and to others. I came to refrain from asking for love or attention, though I wanted it not less. I suppose that in early years you had not time or energy to see all that; later, matters had gone too far.

We lived many places in the Bronx: earliest, a long, roomy apartment, way up high. In it, a corner room facing Crotona Parkway, lace curtains brightly sunlit. This was the "good" parlor and it was my room, when sick. Uncles and aunts and "bubbe" passed through that apartment on the way to their American destinies. From the floor of the everyday living room, when well, I looked up at the knees and distant faces of relatives and a round, dark table that centered everyone. I remember that the building number was 1932; it seemed a shame (this was maybe 1927) that we could not stay until 1932.

Briefly, we lived by ourselves in a semi-basement in an apartment building opposite the entrance to Bronx Park. I rather liked that apartment. There were nooks and crannies and entrance and exit through windows as well as a back and front door, but burglars also discovered this. Then we lived with Uncle Louis. The good parlor was occupied by his daughter. The arrangement must have helped our finances a good deal, but through shut doors I heard you argue with Uncle—almost certainly about me. He thought I was mean to his infant daughter. I was not to enter the front parlor under any circumstances. It is significant, as one says in the business, that I can't remember the layout of the place or where I slept.

If we moved often, it was partly to try to settle our living arrangement and partly because one could negotiate an initial concession (free rent) for a month or two in signing a lease. We lived in a tiny, ground-floor apartment near Crotona Park—dimly lit even with electric lights, protected, a place to eat and sleep. You slept on a couch in the living room. We moved to a roomier five-story walk-up, nearer the subway. And then we joined your widowed sister in a large apartment further around the park. Now the subway roared and screeched to a stop just outside our window—to us as the whir of crickets to a country dweller.

Finally we moved to the last place where you and my brother and I were to live together—in the West Bronx! a step up, a good neighborhood. We three were quite nervous about being closeted together. There would not be other family to buffer our contact; even I was too old now to be involved in the immediate neighborhood. I remember that some wall gadget seemed not to work, and I wanted to cry.

Crotona Park had been like a theater for me—a silent and unpeopled stage lending itself to my designs. I dug into its ground to bake "mickies." I played checkers on the benches and loitered in the grandstand. One night a man who hung around with us slipped his hand gently into my trousers. I spent desperately stormy, solitary nights afterwards trying to arrange the feelings that seized me—avid, ashamed, outraged; and steered clear of him. I kicked my way through drifts of autumn leaves to school. I found canceled checks scattered across a path and hurried home with them, to be told that all the banks had closed. This became my picture of the Depression: Checks were worthless! Later, I was to lie during sweet and, everything considered, innocent evenings on the grass with my girlfriend; once, she asked how I could wonder whether she loved me.

The routines and dramas of my life made a psychological landscape of the park, and it developed a density and texture that only I knew. It was an open space, its boundaries and physical qualities given, otherwise compliant. In my mind it was shaped, filled, furnished with scenarios which, in overlapping, were enriched.

To the five-story walk-up one afternoon came the social worker. She asked for you, I admitted her, and in your absence uneasily answered some questions. Apparently, I said that because you worked I didn't get enough attention. In turn, she threatened you with losing your $25 a month mother's pension (later called Aid to Dependent Children) unless you took better care of me. Indeed, you were really not supposed to be working. You were alarmed and chided me almost helplessly; this was a problem you didn't need to have. And I understood, first, that this well-meaning grown-up social worker was a fool; second, that what I did and said could affect grown-up affairs—such a discovery!; and third, that I had gotten back at you. Still, these were serious matters and I would not again thoughtlessly endanger our welfare.

As an adult professional, I understood that in this way I must have earned designation as a child requiring the city's benign supervision. (Or possibly this was because I was a ward of the court, guardian of the $1,000 held for me from that automobile accident. It helped pay for my graduate degree.) On another visit, the social worker discovered a brand-new copy of *Van Loon's Geography*, $3.75, bought by you after long, thoughtful consideration for my birthday. I knew what a gift it was and have it still, but the social worker wanted to know whether it was a sound expenditure in our circumstances. On the other hand, did it mean that you had sources of income that were not being disclosed?

Years afterward, speaking to assembled administrators of New York City's welfare programs, I showed them the book to make a point about common sense and humility in the conduct of their work. It had been carefully arranged that you should be in that audience. I hope you understood that I was trying to right that particular indignity offered to you. Of course, these early experiences figured in your reaction when, in time, I made my announcement that I would be a social worker.

There was the night when, perhaps eight or nine years old, I lay on my bed waiting for you to come home. Poised between fear of being alone at night and anger that you would stay out so long, I decided to look for you at Uncle Louis's. This meant a walk down Boston Post Road, the elevated train overhead and vast garages on either side, dark in patches; across the West Farms terminus, with brightly lit streetcars at rest or drawing up; over the old industrial bridge across the Bronx River; along the silent, dimly lit margin of Bronx Park; and into the familiar street where my aunt and uncle lived. When they did not answer the bell, I found the door open and walked into the dark living room. Then my aunt appeared in a nightgown, un-accountably stern and unconcerned about me, and said briskly that no, she had not seen you for hours; I would probably find you at home. (Were there no telephones? I guess not yet for us.) I was not angry. Plainly the bedroom from which she emerged held an enigma; perhaps she and Uncle Louis had been having a very serious discussion.

And so I skirted the park again, peered at the Bronx River between the girders of the bridge, crossed West Farms now more silent, went up Boston Road, and to our own place. It was a warm night and I was at home in it, with a pleasant, excited edge of discovery, but both worried that you would now be angry at me and afraid to be alone in the apartment. With every bulb lit, I fell asleep before you came and there was not much talk about the matter the next day, after all. Of course you heard from your sister, and of course I had made my point.

Never spoken between us was the nature of your relationship with Dr. Boorstein. To me he seemed a commanding figure, full of knowledge and power, hurried because so important. He was kind to me from a vast height. I had some reason to be angry at him—his relationship with you and, on various occasions, necessarily, he hurt me—but anger at him was barely sensed before dismissed. Others have said that he was divorced because difficult to live with—egotistical, tyrannical. I do not know whether that was just and, in any event, whether that was how you saw him. You would not entirely have been a patsy.

You spent as much time as you could spare with him and others on Zionist matters. Only once or twice that I recall were we all together on purely social occasions. In his study he had a stereopticon that offered three-dimensional views of foreign cities. I supposed that the capacity to leave such a thing carelessly on one's desk indicated a degree of wealth. Clearly, there was some thought of getting married. Eventually, you let me know that you had decided against marriage because it would not be good for your sons. Mixed with feeling a certain satisfaction, I remember thinking that perhaps it *would* be good for your sons. I did not want the burden of such a favor from you. And indeed I wished you a kind of happiness I sensed you had missed. But day by day, when I felt neglected, it was not your work that I resented but that you were with Dr. Boorstein or engaged in what seemed to me some other self-indulgence.

You could not blame me for being sick and all the rest, but in striking out, as in talking carelessly to the social worker or going alone at night to your sister's house, it must have seemed that I added to your burdens in ways wholly unnecessary. Still, I was lame and needful. Just as I had mixed feelings about Dr. Boorstein—he hurt me, but for my own good and, anyway, in

an adult world defensibly—you must have been angry at me
but unable to harbor the emotion very long. So were we kept in
orbit with each other, tied by need and duty and love, and
distanced by unspoken anger and pride.

Later, it was clear that your relationship with him became
different—not so close, troubled but important. I was urged to
call him when home from school or to pay my respects in some
way. I had no sense that he cared about that, nor any feeling of
what lay between you two that I would, in some fashion, be
affirming or qualifying.

I must have been about ten when I was sent to summer camp—
thought to be good for me but more terrifying than kindergarten because of distance and duration. Fortunately, Uncle Srolik
was a counselor there and, as in hospital, I had a sense of being
an insider. As it turned out, my uncle fell in love with another
counselor. At the very wrong moment I was a responsibility
added to his other duties which, it has to be judged, he bore
with the greatest good will and good humor. In pausing over
his problem, I delay facing my problems at camp—finding
friends, adapting to activities involving skills I did not have,
wondering how to behave, and always certain I was being
judged. Worst was having no time or place to withdraw and
heal. Camp was a trial to be endured, and I endured it. I do
fondly remember the workers' songs sung in Yiddish, the smell
of pine needles, the giant copper sun rolling as it seemed down
a wooded hillside. Such memories are a tribute to the capacity
of time to settle a pink haze over all.

At fourteen or so, I had another operation. Dr. Boorstein clev-
erly explained that this was so I would be able to drive one day.
(*So you can be an astronaut!*, one might extravagantly say today.)
I spent a solitary summer in the five-story walk-up, not unpleasant. Saturday was the high point of the week. I would take
myself on crutches down the hill to the streetcar and thence to

Fordham Hospital to see Dr. Boorstein. Having had my leg handled, a reassuring word or two, and a friendly reference to you, Mother, I would take a streetcar back the other way. Just opposite 1932, the streetcar would let me off at a delicatessen where I had a corned beef sandwich and cream soda—the same every Saturday. And then across the wide boulevard to a movie house that should have been called the Oriental Palace, for how it seemed to me, but carried the given name of some Loew wife or daughter. Nelson Eddy as a Canadian mountie stands tall and sings forth in my memory. Then the long toil with crutches up the hill and up the stairs. It was tiring but worth it and I savored the day's pleasures.

How did I spend my time that summer? Reading, listening to the radio, making a scrapbook, thinking. I thought about God again (having declined to be bar mitzvah, another crisis between us) and gave Him tests, which either He dismissed or failed. Occasionally friends came and we played poker, though I worried that you might not like that. Things were briefly somewhat better for us—money a little easier, the social worker gone along with her $25 a month, and somehow no special tension.

The next summer I walked the length of industrial Third Avenue, entering every shop and asking for any job. Mister Eggers, an electrician, offered me $6 a week—quite a lot of money. He sat me down with an electric fan and asked me to fix it. I spent a day on it without penetrating the steel case; this was one disappointment. He offered to teach me to be an electrician. I said no, thanks, I was going to be a newspaperman. This was a second disappointment, not to say a stupidity. I had said I could type and, assigned to type a postcard for Mr. Eggers, took a whole day to do it—badly. I went to camp for two weeks without telling him and placidly reappeared for work; and he let me. I can only conclude that he had no children and hoped to find one off the street, and was a very patient man, withal.

Needless to say, the machines, and the disarray with its recesses among the crowded stocks of exotic parts, and the smell of oil delighted me. Among my habits at the time was that I would not wear underwear, feeling that this was simple and masculine. With my clothes saturated with oil and dirt, I developed severe boils that kept me out of work again. You remember that you totted it up: Taking medicine and the doctor's bill into account, we experienced a net loss on the enterprise. Nevertheless, I was a workingman!

I reminded you about Mr. Eggers once when you ever so cautiously said what you thought about young people today, blacks in particular. I must have seemed hopeless to Mr. Eggers; nor did I learn anything at all from his tolerance and skill. I lodged for a moment in his world and, for reasons of his own, he let me, but I was a kid and he could not take me anywhere I was going.

In the outside world to which I was turning were teachers. In grade school I remember sharply, as in a snapshot, the nature teacher who told us that birds of prey go by choice for the rump because (striking his backside) it is dependably soft. It was a moment of perfect lucidity, the only time until then and for a long time afterward that I heard my body talked about naturally. His was an unexpected insight; I was also impressed by uninvited generosity. A French teacher asked me to stay after class and gently implied that I did not dress properly. What were my circumstances? It turned out that her husband was a clothing manufacturer, and a couple of weeks later she brought me a pair of trousers. Also, she instructed me how to iron them. This was hardly necessary, for he must have invented indestructible fabric and permapress to meet the specifications she gave. I was a little embarrassed—and you somewhat more—but overcome at the caring.

High school, in addition to students who were to become my lifelong friends, was filled with characters and active minds.

There was Mr. Zieph (that was his name—what was he to do?), brusque, impatient, searching out in any student the argument he would be willing to make; Mr. Sexton, sensitive, language-loving, WASPish (what was he doing in a school of East European Jews and Italian Catholics?); Miss Vermilya, prim, straight, a lover of logic and mathematics; Mrs. Schaaf, my patron, a figure as well as a teacher of romance; Mr. Shamas (did Dickens hire the teachers?), a booming, football player of a speech teacher.

In all the years that I have wondered about the question that a little while ago I asked you (what was the source of my capacity for love and friendship?), it has only lately come clear to me that I was surrounded by relatives and other people who were well disposed, willing to be engaged, and not infrequently more generous than anyone could require.

In 1939, you embarked on a pilgrimage to Chicago and Los Angeles to visit family members barely remembered—including a not till then mentioned Communist cousin. It was the first break in long years of work, a lavish spending of carefully assembled money. Excited postcards marked your progress across the country, and a final postcard said when you would return. It did not occur to me to meet you at the railroad station or make a fuss. I had come to think that you had requirements of me and took pleasure in my progress, but needed little for yourself from me. Instead, you were hurt and angry in a way I had not often seen. (Where was my brother, I wonder—working, and that an acceptable excuse?, or were you also angry at him?) You said, broadening the argument, that I was wasting my time and not justifying your efforts to see me through college. If this went on, you would not. I was shaken.

Perhaps it would have been different if your trip had come earlier. For me it was a time of opening up. I was at summer school and, though I spent little time, in my head absorbed in it. I went every two or three days to the New York World's Fair

and soaked up the spacious, well-ordered world we would
have tomorrow; the presumably naked dancer behind her bub-
bles (truculently permitted by Mayor La Guardia); Judy Gar-
land in high heels and a glittering black dress, red hair piled
like a confection, striding to the crowd; paintings assembled
from around the world, my first sight of El Greco.

Intermitting with my girlfriend, as was my habit, I was
absorbed with Eve. This was a sexual infatuation not quite to
be consummated, and it held me while it held me. And I was
engaged with friends—not simply as part of a crowd anymore—in arguments and ping pong and coming and going, in
sorting out relationships, in walking and standing and lying on
the grass and walking again. I felt fully occupied, fully used.

If I had been less turned outside (but this was the necessity
of my time of life), I might have recognized that you wanted
something for yourself from me. Could I have provided it?
Maybe not, in any case. This was a possibly critical moment and
we missed it; I missed it.

Sex is a matter we never talked about, though you may notice
that I have touched on it several times. I do not think we need
to explore it now, but there are one or two simple things you
should know. I was innocent, as boys and young men go. To
ordinary uncertainty about sexual matters, I added general
social awkwardness and shyness and a desperate unwilling-
ness to open myself to slight. You were yourself, to outward
appearances, prim and inhibited, and there must have been in
your mind a special worry about me: At one point, I turned up
with albumin in my urine and the specialist, uncomfortably
addressing himself to me, suggested that it might be because I
masturbated. In the background of all the (as it turned out)
unnecessary anxiety was the fact, then not known to me, that
my father had died of kidney disease. So perhaps too simply
put, you were worried that I would kill myself masturbating. I
am grateful not to have figured this out until long afterward.

It all flared up between us like sunspots one afternoon when I half-lay on the bed in my room, talking intimately to Norma, who leaned over me. You looked in, blanched, and turned sharply away. This effectively ended the conversation and a few minutes later she left. We radiated sexuality, my friends and I, because of our age and control. But we were as innocent as one might expect. You were cold and contemptuous. This kind of behavior was what would lead you to requiring that I leave school. For my part, I was of course worried about your reaction but also outraged. I knew you were wrong. It all happened in fifteen minutes, and we never spoke about it.

Occasionally, you would ask why I didn't bring friends to the house. I couldn't handle it. One set of relationships at a time occupied me fully.

I was told once that you listed the three men who were important in your life: my brother; David Ben Gurion, prime minister of the State of Israel; and Edward R. Murrow.* I was grown and should have been unsurprised and little affected by my absence from the list, but it was like a blow. I never brought myself to confront you about it; the very question would have disclosed that I minded. I had my own explanation, that you were a snob. Also, you too had ways of paying me back.

Some years after you died, on a family occasion at which there was much reminiscing, Uncle Noftali took me aside to tell me how he had tried to help care for me when I was a baby. I knew this and was fond of him for other reasons as well. But the confidence he really wanted to offer was that, when I was a baby, you had never liked me. It perplexed him. He couldn't

---

*My brother, Dan Schorr, worked with Edward R. Murrow for a period. Dan lived in Europe for many years and, representing him, so to speak, Murrow would send my mother flowers on Mother's Day and perform other small kindnesses. Obviously, she was grateful.

understand why and asked you once, but you were not in the habit of accounting to a younger brother.

Theories about why you might have felt like this came readily to mind: A palpable incompatibility between us from babyhood? This happens. An unwanted child? With a husband critically ill, who needed another child to care for, especially one who was always sick? There was now no way to know about any of this, of course.

It was immediately clear to me that what Noftali reported had been so. It was a stunning "ah hah!" moment, an epiphany, and it freed me. All my theories about our difficult relationship had ostensibly been intended to absolve you, but it was myself I had been trying to justify. If you did not like me, somehow I must have invited this. If the problem began in infancy, however, the character of our relationship was already in some general way determined. Its basic premises were not established by me. So I had not been or done anything except what, in the circumstances, I perforce was and had to do. I do not doubt that you see this differently but, of course, you saw much of this differently. You too had to be and do what you had to be and do.

Alvin

A Short Account
of a Long Apprenticeship

Obviously, other forces—notably, the time in which I grew up—influenced the course of my work. The time was the Great Depression. I was aware that my aunt was regularly laid off when the millinery manufacturer's "season" ended and that often my mother was at risk of being laid off too. Yet, shielded somehow, I was never pressed to help out.

My friend, Erik, moved with his family to New Jersey to eke out their living as chicken farmers because they couldn't manage at all in New York City. I thought that my friend Maxie's family must have money somewhere because they owned the ramshackle house in which they lived. Yet, no one we knew dressed better or spent more money than anyone else, nor did any of us seem to feel deprived.

It was clear that jobs—which were the *main* issue—were very hard to come by. My Uncle Srolik, an intellectual and a lawyer, worked for many years as a Welfare Department investigator—a job he despised—because it was all he could find. But there was more desperation abroad in the country than I saw immediately around me.

The following scraps from Martha Gellhorn's letters to Harry Hopkins will suggest how deep and widespread distress was. (The White House had commissioned Gellhorn to keep them in touch with the realities of day-to-day living. Imagine that!) She wrote first from Gastonia, North Carolina:

> In many mill villages, evictions have been served; more threatened. These men are in a terrible fix.

(Lord, how barren the language seems: these men are faced by the prospect of hunger and cold and homelessness and of becoming dependent beggars—in their own eyes. What more a man can face, I don't know.)

[From Boston] I could go on and on. It is hard to believe that these conditions exist in a civilized country. I have been going into homes at mealtimes and seeing what they eat. It isn't possible; it isn't enough to begin with. . . .

[And from Camden, New Jersey] The young are as disheartening as any group, more so really. They are apathetic, sinking into a resigned bitterness. . . . They don't believe in man or God, let alone private industry. The only thing that keeps them from suicide is this amazing loss of vitality; they exist.[1]

Where I grew up, it was a time of bleak personal prospects but public utopianism and activism. Years later, I argued that an experience of shared difficulty that can be overcome by joint effort leads to a sense of community.[2] For us, at that time, such a sense of community went so deep and was so widely felt that it was never questioned.

The issue was not whether to act but what sort of action to take; my earliest introduction was to a variety of deeply held views about improving the situation of Jews. (Jews were commonly discriminated against in employment, in college admissions and in where they could live, as well as in lesser ways.) Earliest, I heard about General Zionism (my mother), Labor Zionism (my Uncle Noftali) and Revisionism (my Uncle Morris). These were, respectively, militant, more militant and "only by armed conflict" positions about how to establish a Jewish state in Palestine.

In high school, in the years leading to the rise of Hitler and to World War II, I was president of the American Student Union. Like much of the country, we students were confirmed pacifists, opposed to being caught up in a war in Europe. I led a "Peace Strike" march at the school, prompting a story in the Hearst *Journal American* with the streamer headline, "Evander Childs High School, A Hotbed of Communism." My recollection is that we were more charmed by this moment of fame than alarmed by its wild mischaracterization. Along with others, however, I was called into the principal's office to watch him scrawl in red letters across my record card, "Peace Strike, 1938." The implicit threat was that this would keep us out of college.

Admissions to City College would have declined considerably if the college had been deterred by such considerations. Attendance there immersed me in an argument, mostly outside of classrooms, that was broader than Zionism: what to do about our society as a whole. In hangouts reserved for students, one could find belligerent protagonists for any position—Social Democratic, Socialist, Young People's Socialist League, Young Communist League, Trotskyite, Lovestonite. It was understood, scornfully, that the engineering students would *not* get involved; for the rest of us, it was regarded as human nature to be involved.

Many faculty members were deeply engaged with the students. English was my "major," though I took no electives in it. In an introductory class, Prof. William G. Crane asked us to write a short essay. When I handed in my paper after twenty minutes and turned to leave, he said *he* couldn't do a satisfactory paper in twenty minutes. Unable to resist a straight line, I said "maybe *you* couldn't" and went on my way. At the next class, he invited me to do assigned papers, which we would discuss in his office, and excused me from attending classes. Milton Millhauser taught literature and enrolled me in the National Youth Administration (NYA, a New Deal program for college students) so I could be paid fifty cents an hour for checking references in his doctoral dissertation on the Italian Risorgimento. I came to think NYA was a "make-work" program and, of course, it was, but the fifty cents an hour paid for carfare or lunch and a date or two.

As it turned out, I took most of my electives in an honors sequence in psychology. Perhaps this was an indication that I was headed not for journalism, which majoring in English was meant to advance, but for something more inward looking. But I found time to work on the campus newspaper.

Among psychology professors, I remember Gardner Murphy, the "star" lured up the street from Columbia University; Isidor Chein, cited along with Kenneth Clark in the 1954 Supreme Court decision on school desegregation; Walter Neff and Joseph E. Barmack. These people were all heatedly engaged in their work, and they opened our minds to its excitement.

Among other important influences, I mention the effect of being Jewish. In time, I came to believe that all professions are prisons, impeding communication with our peers and empathy with our clients. The valuable people in dissolving such barriers are marginal people—psychiatrists, poets, expatriates, comedians, blacks, Jews. Sources and effects of marginality are elusive; I quote Thorstein Veblen:

> [A Jew pays] the cost of losing his secure place in the scheme of conventions into which he has been born, and . . . of finding no similarly secure place in the scheme of gentile conventions into which he is thrown. . . . He is in a peculiar degree exposed to the unmediated facts of the current situation; and takes his orientation from the run of facts as he finds them, rather than from the traditional interpretation. . . .[3]

Veblen was writing of European Jews almost eighty years ago. Nevertheless, I recognize this effect. I was rarely wholly captured by an institution or an establishment point of view—

even those I earnestly espoused. Like an anthropologist, in some corner of my mind I observed and doubted and measured and tested. What everyone agreed upon and fervently declared was inherently suspect. Naturally, I was therefore often not on the popular side of an issue.

Having settled on social work by a process that is no longer clear to me, if it ever was clear, but tangentially involving a professor who had once taught in a social work school, I applied for admission to three graduate schools of social work. Columbia University turned me down because I was not old enough or experienced enough. Western Reserve University—I had a cousin in Cleveland—required a *nonrefundable $5* application fee. I thought this a scam and declined to pursue the application. Washington University in St. Louis—where my professor had taught—accepted me.

In retrospect, it all seems haphazard; surely, I must have been more thoughtful than I now recall? In any event, I have come to think that I would have found my way to some mix of social policy and writing, no matter what route I took.

Graduate School

I went off to the George Warren Brown School of Social Work, Washington University, in St. Louis—somewhat anxious but also excited. I had my first glimpse of real-life cows and pigs from the train window. (Now, of course, one can see them in the Bronx Zoo.) I took this sighting to confirm that a whole new world awaited me.

Housed in a simple but classy dormitory room, I felt at ease in the long days that stretched out before me. (Classes were a three-minute walk away, in contrast to the hour or so by street-car or subway to which I was accustomed.) The campus was spacious, covered with grass and alight with flowers. I had little idea what social work would be, but found myself comfortable in studying it. From the start, it was less taxing than under-graduate work.

The professors were okay. Some of them were characters—that is, fanatic about research design with students few of whom would ever do research, or so deeply immersed in psychoanalytic thinking as to confuse metaphors with real life, or so professional as to overlook the role of ordinary human warmth in our work—but this was also okay. Such fixations may have been necessary for teaching, I now think. Even so, like the professors at City College, they seemed to care a great deal about their students.

I thought I might want to be like one in particular—Benjamin Youngdahl, a professor for whom social work and reform were a single idea. Although I never took his class, I understood what he was about. In time, we became friends. Many years later, by a considerable coincidence, *my* son wound up working in *his* son's labor relations law firm (representing trade unions and employees) in Little Rock, Arkansas.

The workload was light and, by the last semester, I was able to arrange my schedule so I could complete all my work between Tuesday and Thursday. I spent the long weekends with a girlfriend or simply floating along in this new, Midwestern style. I thought this was going to be the softest period in my whole life. However, I was still ill at ease socially. No doubt, this accounted for a certain brashness and prankishness which fellow alumni occasionally recall.

Notwithstanding the light workload, I emerged from graduate school having absorbed convictions about professionalism and ethical behavior that have never left me. I learned how to counsel people in difficulty without trying to shape them to be like me. And I absorbed an optimistic, expansionist view of the future of the social work profession.

In 1941, social work was not greatly valued among professions—a woman's profession, as my mother had said, with low pay, identified with welfare, and, in many settings, subordinate to physicians—but it was clear to our professors and so to us that we were entrusted with an irresistible engine that integrated ideas about psychotherapy, family relations and community into a single service. These would win us a valued place in the new world we would help to make.

My first year in graduate school was the year that the Japanese attacked the U.S. fleet in Pearl Harbor. We were, perforce, at war in the Far East and Europe; it was to be the last "popular" war in recent history. Friends and fellow students and one or two faculty members went off to the military. Not being involved was hard. I tried to enlist—without success, of course: My leg, atrophied because of polio, would not get me past a physical examination.

The atmosphere on campus was strange. Millions of people were torn up and apart by the war but, except for the absence of male students from classes and the not terribly onerous rationing of cigarettes, gasoline and some foods, there was little evidence of change. Rather it felt, to me at any rate, as if we were sidelined. I volunteered my social work skills, such as they so far were, to gather from draftees medical and social information that induction stations wanted to have.

The career ladder for people who intended to be administrators, as I did, was to work as a social caseworker, advance to supervisor of other caseworkers, become administrator in a small agency and eventually wind up as executive of a medium- or large-size agency. This could take five years or twenty, depending on talent, luck and how driven one was.

On graduation, I thought that I would return to New York to start this ascent. However, three or four interviews there suggested that it would take me forever to get anywhere. One interviewer said that after three years I might be promoted to doing casework with *new* clients!—*if I showed promise!*

And So to Work

I therefore called the executive of Family Service of St. Louis County, Philip Akre, whom I had known at school. He had offered me a job and now I was willing to take it. I worked in his agency, counseling people with marital problems, problems with children, money management problems and so forth for about three years. The work was interesting, but I was not distinguishing myself or making any progress.

In retrospect, it is plain that my interest and talents lay elsewhere than in casework itself. Applying untapped energy, in St. Louis several colleagues and I undertook to enlist the staff in a trade union. I knew next to nothing about organizing a union, but our salaries were so low that almost everyone signed up. We had a little help from the St. Louis Labor Council and did, indeed, win a respectable raise.

I moved along to a job as psychiatric social worker (a title more prestigious than caseworker) with the Veterans Administration in New Jersey, where at least I would earn more money. In this position, I regularly saw veterans who were living in the community on "trial visit" from a V.A. mental hospital. I helped with the adjustments to living outside a hospital with which they were struggling.

I recall quite clearly a patient in Atlantic City—fifty years later, I even remember his name—who would not talk to me at all until I hit upon the device of playing chess with him. His paranoid inclinations gave him a considerable advantage, I thought, and I regarded it as a triumph to win a game. After some contact with each veteran, I would arrive at a careful judgment about how he (there were no women in my caseload) was managing and make a recommendation to the hospital about ending or extending his trial visit.

After 1946, the Veterans Administration was raising its professional standards and expanding. General Omar Bradley, who had been named V.A. administrator, was bent on delivering the best possible care to returning veterans. Here (displaying what was to become a pattern—that is, finding an activity other than casework and writing about it, besides) I was drawn into starting a newsletter for V.A. social workers. When it was well established, I wrote editorials promoting an independent social work department which would not be subordinate to physicians. Ah, well!, we shall see such independence for social workers in a medical facility when—as the Arabic saying goes —apricots bloom in the desert.

After three years or so at V.A., I moved to the Prince Georges County (Maryland) Welfare Board as one of two supervisors. In a large county adjacent to Washington, D.C., this agency provided cash assistance and, for abused and neglected children and their families, a variety of social services. It was a local office of the Maryland State Board of Public Welfare, then one of the nation's best state programs.

We were given clear objectives that were focused on helping clients. Staff were mainly young college graduates, with a strong sense of mission; the quality of the work they were able to do left me unable thereafter to be patronizing about "untrained" social workers. I found myself for the first time in a job that largely occupied my energy and imagination. (I say "largely" because in this period I met my wife and married and was thinking of much else, as well.)

My pleasure in the job was not to last. The director retired and was succeeded by a woman who undertook to turn the agency towards "rehabilitating" its clients. This was all right, in principle, but she defined rehabilitation in a way that proved to be forty years ahead of her time: Her idea was to terminate welfare or return children to their parents and simply tell them that they could get by. When caseworkers declined to behave like this, she would ask clients into her office and, in two-hour sessions, persuade them (and sometimes she did persuade them) that she was terminating their assistance for their own good.

Since much that she did was contrary to law and regulations, not to mention damaging to clients, I supported workers who resisted her instructions. When state auditors picked up on violations of law, she instructed workers to alter their records. Again, I supported the workers, but obviously the situation could not go on. I took occasion to talk to the businessman who chaired the county welfare board, and he counseled patience. He added thoughtfully that if he had a gas station and it was making money, he would not interfere with the manager.

One day, the director called me into her office and dismissed me. I grasped the depth of her rage when, upon leaving her office, I placed a call to the state welfare office. Before seeing me, she had instructed the switchboard operator not to complete any calls for me.

Actually, I thought she was clinically ill—impulsive, sent out of control by resistance of any sort, not clear about reality. Some months after I left, she physically assaulted a worker who contradicted her and was dismissed herself. This was too late to be of use to me. My wife and I had planned to live on one of our salaries for two years and then travel around the world, but this was now out of the question.

Indeed, I worried that my career had been blighted before it was well begun. I need not have fretted; over the years, I have known a number of prominent social workers who went on from dismissal to better jobs—whatever one makes of that. The ladder seems to go up, no matter how sound the rung one steps off from. The state director of public welfare volunteered to provide a work reference for me, somewhat moderating my anxiety.

Moving up the ladder myself, upon referral from a placement agency, I now accepted a position as director of United Charities of West Hazleton (Pennsylvania). United Charities was a small philanthropic organization that provided counseling for families and versatile services for children: a small children's home, foster care, adoption and services to children in their own homes. The organization was old and well established, but somewhat neglected and not quite modern in its practices. For example, although it was well understood that children do not belong in an institution unless there is a special reason, children who entered the children's home tended to stay for extended periods.

Much was new to me—being director, dealing with a board and running a children's home—and I entered upon it all with verve. There were unanticipated problems. For example, I had not been taught in school what to do when the furnace in a children's home breaks down and a repairman is not available.

Also, in interviewing me the board had neglected to mention that the prior executive fell in love with a teenager in the children's home and married her. Her younger sister was still in the institution. (This was in another age: The marriage notwithstanding, it was a considerable scandal.) This history explained how warily I was regarded when I walked around the children's home, and the disingenuous questions at the Rotary Club about how things were going. But for several weeks I did not understand.

I recall my first Christmas at United Charities. The first Jewish executive since it was founded fifty years earlier, I was determined that the children in our care would nevertheless not be stinted at Christmastime. I shopped for Christmas decorations myself and, at a paper goods supplier, was asked if I wanted a crèche. At my puzzled look, the salesman asked in Yiddish: *Yir weisst nisht vos is a crèche?!* (You don't know what a crèche is?!) The children wrote letters to Santa; we passed them on to Rotary and Kiwanis members, who bought lavish gifts and delivered them to us to give to the children. Never was there such a Christmas! Given a choice, the children would not have gone back to having a Christian director. (At my school of social work, there would have been much analysis of my motivation in doing all this: *Was I trying to buy the children's approval?*)

At any rate, as any new director will, I set out to improve things. At some financial cost to us (because the county paid a per diem rate for children in the home), we moved children for whom it was appropriate back to their own homes or into family foster homes. We replaced the ailing furnace, converted dormitory space into private rooms for older children and redecorated the children's home. We "marketed" our services better, as one would say now, so that more people came to us for help. I learned the curious lesson that donors are more likely to give to a charity that seems to be doing well. In a good or even in a bad cause, prosperity sells. Pathos does not sell.

Hazleton was developed as a company town—small, wood frame houses, crowded side by side—set among spectacular mountains, on the edge of the Poconos. The owners of the anthracite coal mines, who built and mined Hazleton, had moved on to New York and other cosmopolitan centers, taking their foundations and charitable gifts with them. (The reader may detect a remembered bitterness: It did not seem fair that they should take so much and leave so little.) The mines were worked out. Women worked in garment and shoe factories that had escaped the unions in New York. Men did what they could.

Conyngham, the nearby tiny village where we lived, lies nestled among tree-covered mountains—green much of the year and sparkling white with snow in the winter. Two of our children were born in the State's "Miners' Hospital" in Hazleton. *They* saw cows across the street and played in the brook that ran alongside our apartment.

Still, Hazleton was a small place and I had done what I could at United Charities. At more or less the right moment, the Family Service Association of America (FSAA)—a national organization of agencies such as United Charities, with which I frequently consulted—offered me a position as director of a demonstration project in southern Ohio, and I accepted it. (Although there was no way to know this, I was now pointed towards a government job that would offer a quantum leap in responsibility and moving-around room.)

In 1954, the Goodyear Atomic Corporation was building a $2 billion atomic energy plant for the government in southern Ohio. Thousands of construction workers with their families, one hundred thousand people in all, were moving into a poor, rural three-county area, doubling the counties' population.

They worked on their jobs, lived in trailers for four or five months and moved on. Considerable social dislocation was anticipated; trailer families were generally thought to be rootless, with shallow relationships, not invested in the community.

A national agency called United Community Defense Services (UCDS) organized social services for civilians affected by national defense activities. FSAA proposed to establish a family counseling agency for UCDS that would serve the needs of these presumably troubled families and the families of the rural, underserved area as well. Perhaps, we could even develop a model for providing in rural areas the type of family services that were typically found in urban areas.

We had quite a good time in Waverly, Ohio. It was a frontier town: only one hotel (but it had been modernized to have a bathroom on every floor!), party-line telephones, no metropolitan newspaper delivery and no television reception worth struggling for. Yet, in this high-priority national defense area, roads were laid in a day or two and housing sprang up on vacant lots like flowers after a spring rain. The domestic creatures that our children learned to identify now were bulldozers, backhoe loaders, cement trucks.

For the people who would stay on after construction was completed, the federal government had guaranteed loans for one thousand prefabricated houses—built on a slab, one story. My wife and I had never owned a house and these looked pretty good to us. One could not buy a house without a government priority and, accorded a priority, we bought one. It quickly turned out that the houses were sloppily constructed and no one wanted them. I asked the Federal Housing Authority (FHA) regional representative why they had authorized so many "permanent" houses. He said: *The Dems had their turn. Now it is our turn.* (Democratic President Harry S. Truman had been succeeded by Republican President Dwight D. Eisenhower.)

Exploration made it clear that a flim-flam had been organized from the beginning. The construction company built the homes for a management company; both companies had the same corporate officers. The management company paid off the construction company, which disappeared from the scene. With many houses unsold and vacant, the management company went into bankruptcy. (Having guaranteed the construction loans, FHA took the loss.) It appeared that there was no corporate entity that we could hold responsible.

I gathered together the individual owners and we wrote to Washington. It was obvious that the homes did not meet building specifications. We met with management company officers and threatened to ask for inspections by FHA and to go to the newspapers. The officers offered to repurchase the houses at the price that we had paid and then rent them to us; and I accepted. They were entirely cheerful about it. While we were engaged in negotiations, they commented on how effectively I was representing the purchasers and offered me a job—a common ploy in business, apparently. Not every owner was happy; some wanted more than they had paid and suspected that I had sold them out. I invited them to decline to sell.

At the Family Service Association, we found ourselves in the company of staff from other national organizations, all with a high level of competence and dedication, who were helping to build a structure for what was essentially a new community. I remember particularly Mary Miller, from the Girl Scouts, and John Gensel, from the Lutheran Mission. I spent one early morning with Gensel on a truck delivering milk, though I do not now recall why. There was considerable camaraderie and sharing of ideas about what must be done.

We set about systematically establishing a family service agency and a basis for it to continue. In a few months, we had three local committees that advised and sponsored us, including a federal judge, the deputy director of Goodyear Atomic Corporation, a local minister, a lay Girl Scout leader and so forth. We publicized the counseling service; in a year over a hundred items about us appeared in local newspapers. We composed a personal advice column for one local newspaper, but dropped it when no one wrote to us for advice. Writing a successful advice column is not as easy as it may seem. In any event, people began to come in for counseling.

There were other experiences that reflected the frontier quality of the area. Told that a family wanted our help, Martha Van Valen, our caseworker, traveled down a dirt road that faded away at a trailer. No one was at home and she left a card with a message offering to help. A couple of days later, we received a response: "We don't have any problems that couldn't be straightened out with a bulldozer."

For a little while, rumbles of thunder and wisps of smoke had emanated from New York, where, in those years, national funding organizations like UCDS, FSAA and Community Chests and Councils of America (now United Way) herded together and plotted and planned. We did not pay much attention until, maybe eighteen months into what we had hoped would be a three-year project, we were told that our funding had ended. We must fold up.

With less than two years in the field, it would have been hard to be convincing about the conclusions that we were, in fact, drawing. Was such a family service useful in a rural, changing, "defense impacted" area? Absolutely. Like people everywhere, the population, new and old, had family problems and the old population had problems of poverty with which we could and did help. Did our circuit-riding social workers and nascent three-county board of directors provide a model that might be successful? No. We had not found sources of serious, ongoing financial support anywhere.

We arrived at the answer to one question that it had not occurred to us to ask. Contrary to conventional wisdom, these trailer families were generally stable, with well-developed coping skills. Although they expected to be in the area only a few months, for example, they often extended a canopy from their trailers, doubling their usable living area, and planted flowers and even *trees* at strategic points. Their children joined the Girl Scouts and went to church and what other activities were available. They lived as nearly as seemed possible as if they were going to stay forever. And with relatively good income, they spent freely on making themselves comfortable. My wife and I, who had our own experience in moving about, learned a thing or two from them.

I went now to be director at Family Service of Northern Virginia, a counseling agency that served the Virginia suburbs of Washington, D.C. This was 1956—a nervous period in Virginia. The 1954 U.S. Supreme Court decision on desegregation notwithstanding, Harry Byrd, Virginia's U.S. senator, had declared the state's "massive resistance to this [desegregation] order." "Massive resistance," his biographer wrote, "would mean recourse to all available means to prevent any integration in the Commonwealth."[4]

A black woman was the first of my board members to visit me; we were to discuss the agency's public relations program. She interrupted our opening greetings to say that *I can't do business with you without knowing how you feel about what's going on.* So we talked about race relations and desegregation and got that out of the way. It was relevant that her husband, a newspaperman, was at the center of a bitter controversy about admitting a black to Washington's prestigious Cosmos Club.

To mark our agency's tenth anniversary, we invited Margaret Mead to address our annual meeting on the subject of "The New American Family." (We had a *new* American family then, as now.) We were to meet in a bar near the State Department before going on to our meeting. Mead had spent the day in conferences and, tired, rested her ample frame on a little cocktail table and opened our conversation with: *Now tell me— what made me agree to speak for you?* While I groped for words, she added: *No, let me reconstruct our conversation. You called and asked me to speak and I said I don't speak to segregated audiences. You said it would* not *be segregated; and then I was stuck, wasn't I?*

Later, she gave a fine address. She displayed a picture of Elizabeth Taylor and Mike Todd from a cover story in *Life* magazine in November 1957. They were grouped as an intimate threesome with their three-month-old baby girl. That—the father involved in parenting the baby—was a key aspect of the "new" American family.

As the agency was flourishing, we undertook new projects. Pursuing an educational approach to family problems, we encouraged people with "normal" questions or tensions to make appointments; and we advertised discussion groups about raising children, communication between spouses and so forth. We learned that several children had died in Arlington Hospital, with malnutrition given as the reason for death. When we determined that the children had been in welfare families, we looked into assistance levels and took the matter up with our state legislators. I tried to enlist the help of the county medical society. In the end, the only visible result of this effort was that doctors would no longer list malnutrition as a cause of death.

We got involved in the question of caseworker productivity. In our agency and in agencies like it across the country, a caseworker conducted 2.5 counseling interviews in a typical day. This seemed to me to be not enough. It is true that workers spend time on telephone calls and correspondence and other necessary activities but much time was wasted, as it seemed to me, in dictating verbatim reports of what had been said in interviews. Caseworkers had learned to do this in graduate school, where the record was used for supervision and teaching, but there was no justification for it in professional practice. Nevertheless, dictation was deeply embedded in social work culture and all but impossible to change. I thought it a triumph to bring our average up from 2.5 to three interviews a day in the course of a couple of years.

Meanwhile, I had written about the FSAA demonstration project in southern Ohio. An article arguing that trailer families managed as well as most other families appeared in *Harper's*

Magazine.[5] William L. Mitchell, deputy commissioner of the Social Security Administration, was looking around for someone who could help adapt social security programs to the needs of American families, and the article caught his eye. Presumably, there were discreet inquiries about me and then he invited me to his office for a conversation. His decision to offer me a position opened a door on government policy that I would not have known enough to dream of.

Looking back, I think that the fifteen years I spent in social service agencies—family counseling, mental hygiene, public assistance and child welfare, as caseworker, supervisor and administrator—made an important contribution to the policy work that I subsequently did. I was often impatient, having an inchoate feeling that something lay out there that was bigger and more inventive than I was doing. Yet, I really needed to learn that New York City and Washington University were not the United States and I needed experience in dealing with people who were not in my neighborhood or university.

I learned a respect for casework and everyday work with people that not all policy people have. I saw policies applied in detail and felt more securely grounded in the meanings of legislation and other formal policies because I had seen how they are transmuted and collaged in the real world outside the legislative chamber or board room. This should have been a check on my ambition, when I came to the federal government, to straighten out all the nation's problems from Washington; but it was not.

NOTES

1. Martha Gellhorn, "The Thirties," *Granta*, 23, Spring 1988.

2. Alvin L. Schorr, *Common Decency: Domestic Policies After Reagan*, Yale University Press, New Haven, Connecticut, 1986, Chapter 2.

3. Thorstein Veblen, "The Intellectual Pre-eminence of Jews in Modern Europe," *Political Science Quarterly*, XXXIV, no. 1, March 1919, pp. 39–41.

Erik Erikson made a similar observation in *Childhood and Society,* W. W. Norton, New York, 1950.

Regarding marginality in comedians, see Victor Goertzel and Mildred George Goertzel, *Cradles of Eminence,* Little, Brown & Co., Boston, 1962. Regarding marginality in psychiatrists, see Karl Menninger, *A Psychiatrist's World,* Viking Press, New York, 1959, pp. 415–24, 477–96; and Jurgen Ruesch and Gregory Bateson, *Communication: The Social Matrix of Society,* W. W. Norton, New York, 1951, p. 20. Regarding marginality in blacks, see any work of James Baldwin or Ralph Ellison.

4. Senator Byrd's quotation and the biographer's comment may be found in Ronald L. Heinemann, *Harry Byrd of Virginia,* University Press of Virginia, Charlottesville, 1996, p. 334.

5. Alvin L. Schorr, "Families on Wheels," *Harper's Magazine,* January 1958, pp. 71–75.

American Family Policy: Learning by Doing

In 1958, when William Mitchell invited me to join his staff to work out how social security programs might more usefully serve the American family, I was a practicing social worker—not a researcher or policy expert—and it would have been hard to argue that I was especially qualified for the task. Mitchell must have seen something in me that few others would have seen. For the next seven years, I was to be absorbed in determining how policy might promote two particular objectives: more rewarding family relationships and a reduction in poverty.

The search led to conclusions that proved controversial and often drew powerful opposition. Nevertheless, two commissioners of Social Security authorized publication of the major pieces of my work. As such determination may leave a commissioner exposed, it is not universal. I was trying to show that a free exchange of ideas—within the government as well as without, whether a particular idea wins or loses the day—would make for richer research and sounder government programs. The trial struck me as in some small measure convincing.

The Social Security Administration was an agency of the U.S. Department of Health, Education and Welfare (HEW), now Health and Human Services. I was lodged administratively in the Commissioner's Office of Research and Statistics (ORS)— an office staffed by hard-working, talented economists and statisticians. Out of collegiality and, I suspected, anxiety that in some public statement I might embarrass them, they gave me as I went along a high-intensity if sporadic education in their specialties—particularly the proper uses of statistics.

Central to my choice of how to go about my work was that this was the Eisenhower administration and America had not yet seen the end of Senator Joseph McCarthy's malign influence. Not many years before, the director of ORS had been dismissed—in effect, by Congress—for displaying a too warm interest in national health insurance. Closer to my time Jacob Fisher, another ORS staff member, was dismissed as a security risk. (He later wrote about the episode in an autobiography.[1]) The lessons in such dismissals were widely learned. It was not a time of intellectual ferment or venturesomeness; the rule in government was to avoid attention.

I took this climate to mean, first, that there was a shortage of good ideas and so a market for them; second, that for the moment research (rather than program development or advocacy) was the strategy of choice—even though I knew rather little about it; and third, that such proposals as I might favor ought to draw upon as many sources of authority as possible.

I began, as I noted in the Introduction, with a review of Aid to Dependent Children (ADC). (Later, "families with" was inserted in the name and in its acronym, AFDC.) What reasons did I give for starting with ADC? It was the only program in the Social Security Administration that dealt with families as families; and these were often very troubled families. For perhaps a year, I read hundreds of ADC program studies to see what the reports were saying. Poor design or a researcher bent on making a personal point often blunted a study's message, but grasping the import of all the studies taken together was simply an exercise in attention.

From the beginning, I relied a good deal on intuition and empathy. It was not an accident that the title of a book I produced at the time, *Explorations in Social Policy,* reduces to E.S.P.[2] Word was abroad that amassing data is research, while intuition is merely poetry or clinical practice. The notion reflects an analogy to a science-that-never-was or a technician's flight from the risk of making errors. Intuition must be subjected to trial by data and by theory, of course. However, it is only the glimmering of an idea or of a solution that makes the endless data-collecting bearable.

The report of that work on ADC was the first published declaration by an administration official that the program was in serious trouble. The article dealt with problems in ADC under four headings: "the scapegoat phenomenon," "the work dilemma," "maternal family or whole family?" and "toward stability?"[3] It is interesting now to see how little our predicament about welfare has changed in thirty-five years, despite sweeping changes in social conditions and a succession of highly touted welfare reforms. Some things about ADC *did* change; we will come to that.

A confidential draft of the report on ADC drew bitter and protracted resistance from responsible federal administrators, and they opposed its publication. It has to be said for them that the program was under serious attack in the press and on Capitol Hill for promoting delinquency and illegitimacy. They were afraid that official criticism would lend weight to moves to cut back the program and so would hurt clients. Mitchell needed a way to test the credibility of the report and, at my suggestion, he sent copies to two dozen administrators and scholars outside government. He drew from most of them what may fairly be characterized as "at last!" or "it is high time!" comments. Meanwhile, of course, the existence of the report became informed-circle gossip.

In the end, Mitchell authorized publication, writing testily to the director of the Bureau of Public Assistance that "we have about worn out the use of defensive assertions to off-set critical assertions. If we are to preserve the essential values in ADC, we have got to propose constructive measures. . . ."[4]

I had recommendations to propose—they would be tediously familiar now—about incentives to work, for example, and laid them out for the commissioner. He was fond of me and, so, avuncular in his response (I paraphrase): *Don't you think I know all that, Alvin? The problem is that if I have legislation drafted along these lines, practically no one in the department will support it. If Congress schedules hearings, no official will testify with conviction. Before such a bill can be sent up, the climate has to be prepared so it will have a chance.* This was one of my earliest lessons: Policy is not simply a matter of the excellence of ideas!

Policy control at the time was very tight; on reflection I understood that there would be risk for me if I undertook to prepare the climate without explicit authorization. Yet, if I asked for authorization it would be denied. Deciding to proceed without authorization, I communicated my ideas about the program in private to editors and reporters. (Despite a "personal opinion" disclaimer, the published article[5] lent authority to my views.) I accepted invitations to speak at professional and citizen meetings, translating a careful, footnoted paper into less guarded language and adding suggestions about corrective legislation.

In the months that followed, discussion of incentive arrangements, extending the program to two-parent families, and other ideas blossomed—not simply because I had opened up the subject; rather, I had selected a subject that was fated to be opened up. My hope was to point the inevitable conversation towards constructive solutions.

Meanwhile I began exploring other subjects; there was no lack of ideas. For a time I looked into the issue of interfaith marriage. Young people were widely being counseled that such marriages were risky, though they seemed to contract them anyway. I thought that social scientists were exaggerating negative findings of outcome in interfaith marriage but, in the end, I decided not to get into this. It would have been hard to explain why the government should involve itself.

A more appropriate issue for me might have been family life education; the Children's Bureau and, for that matter, the Department of Agriculture were heavily involved in parent education and I was being urged to lend a hand. After reviewing the research and talking to parent educators, I found myself doubtful that their work improved child-rearing very much.[6] Here too I decided not to get into the matter. People were receiving a service they wanted. Why should I start an argument?

I reflected that studying ADC had not precisely answered to my charge to focus on families. I had started with a program and asked family-outcome questions about it. That was all right, but I concluded that my charge was to go the other way around: to ask a question about family life and then examine the programs that were relevant. Research conducted in such a fashion was rare. To government administrators who sought answers to use in doing business, social scientists came across like solipsists on a retreat.

(I recall, wryly, the example of a small group of distinguished academicians who assembled at our invitation to discuss the relation of social security and families. For a day and a half the meetings made rapid progress toward reaching conclusions. Then, at lunch before the closing session, one of the group, Otto Pollak, offered me a private forecast: *Watch what we do this afternoon. We'll back off; we'll say that a good deal more research is needed before we can feel confident about what we've been saying.* Of course, he was right.[7])

The question that I finally formulated was: What is the nature of the relationship of the elderly and their adult children? If we could answer this question dependably, then we could ask how such relationships are influenced by major government programs like retirement insurance and Old Age Assistance (now Supplemental Security Income). I proceeded in the same manner as I had in studying ADC—reading widely, consulting experts, and using the extensive program statistics developed by the Social Security Administration. There issued from this labor a government pamphlet.[8] (Because it was the agency's first publication with a colored cover, it came to be known as the "purple pamphlet." In the good old days Congress was said to frown on the waste implicit in colored covers.)

This work pointed to a more sanguine view of the family life of aged people than was current in pop sociology. It was the habit—a habit that survives—to mourn the demise of the American family and the consequent abandonment of old people. Though some old people may suffer from such a problem, it was not and is not the common pattern. However, nostalgia and its corollary that everything is getting worse die hard.

This time the report contained a major conclusion that the Bureau of Public Assistance quite liked: Laws requiring adult children to support their aged parents before they can receive Old Age Assistance (so-called "relative responsibility" laws) save little government money but painfully upset family relationships.[9]

On the other hand, the Bureau of Old Age and Survivors Insurance was not charmed by conclusions touching on their turf, such as a very small social security program that provides for aged, dependent parents who are not otherwise entitled to social security. I concluded that this program was so small because the definition of "dependent" was so foreign to the way families behave, even when children *are* helping, that few elderly people applied or even knew about it. However, the bureau was not disposed to spend much energy on the issue. With this report, trouble came from outside.

Returning from a field trip, I found on top of a pile of mail a copy of a syndicated column by Raymond Moley. Moley had been a Roosevelt brain-truster and was now a rightwing think-tanker. It was just after the election in 1960 and his column said this: Conservative voters had not voted for Nixon because of the Eisenhower administration's "indiscriminate employment of [people like Alvin L. Schorr] with extremely radical and visionary notions about . . . welfare and the government's responsibility." Words such as "shocking" and "utter perversion of morality" followed.[10] It was not a time, if there ever is one, when such a charge could be taken lightly.

I had settled myself to consider what to do when the phone

rang; it was Mitchell. The commissioner inquired courteously about my field trip and then asked whether I had seen the Raymond Moley column. "Yes, sir," I said. He said that as I was new to this sort of thing, he would offer advice. It would occur to me to reply but he advised against it. The reply would never catch up with the accusation. Was there other work I was planning to do? Well, yes, I wanted to talk to him about it. He suggested that I proceed with my work.

Twenty years later, at a party in Washington, he asked if I remembered the "purple pamphlet." Another official had given him the message that the secretary of HEW saw Moley's column and wanted me dismissed, but Mitchell was vague about details. Mitchell had been a career civil servant, and I could only speculate how he would have dealt with such an instruction. He may have told the secretary that Moley's was an eccentric reading of the pamphlet. He might have said that I had become well known on university campuses, and dismissing me could draw a reaction. In any case, he would have promised to look into the matter and, eventually, it would have faded away in the press of more important business. I had never heard a word about it.

Fully to grasp Mitchell's integrity, one has to know that a Democratic administration, shortly to take office, was by no means required to reappoint a sitting commissioner, let alone one carried over from a Republican administration. A fracas about an extreme radical and visionary [read, Communist] in his office was the last thing Mitchell needed. There was no fracas that I knew about and, in any case, he was reappointed.

I knew by now that a set of ideas embodied in a publication is merely a first step towards reform, if that. Especially as there was no particular sensitivity about these ideas in my own agency, it was possible to promote them in all ways open to me, including conversations with legislators and newspaper people, speeches and op-ed pieces. The "purple pamphlet" was published not long before the 1961 White House Conference on

Aging, then an influential national forum. The conference used the pamphlet as resource material, decided to support eliminating "relative responsibility" laws with respect to the elderly, and members earnestly lobbied Congress to act on this.

When Congress enacted Medicaid in 1965, it forbade states to incorporate a provision holding adult children liable for their parents' medical expenses. Shortly afterward the New York state legislature, seeking to harmonize the administration of its new Medicaid program with its welfare program, wiped out "relative responsibility" in Old Age Assistance as well as in Medicaid. In 1972, when Congress replaced Old Age Assistance with Supplemental Security Income, it settled the issue. States could no longer require adult children to support their aged parents.

While the Moley column was incubating, I was on a field trip to the scene of some of the first sit-ins of the civil rights movement. How was this within my charge? Like everybody studying welfare, I had been reading about the black family. Certain observations were commonly offered: Blacks did not share majority society values (cohesive families, sacrifice for future gain, planning ahead). Black boys, in particular, grew up undisciplined and irresponsible. The popular phrase for all this was "culture of poverty"; "underclass" had not yet come into favor. Blacks were not *blamed* for "present orientation" and all the rest, not by social scientists, who were given to asserting that they were not judgmental. They explained in exquisite detail how the circumstances of blacks had brought them to this pass.

It struck me that young blacks were exhibiting very considerable planning, discipline and responsibility in conducting sit-ins, and I wondered how this accorded with the theories that filled the pages of professional journals. By all that social scientists knew about it, the sit-in movement should never have happened.[11] If I could understand the discrepancy between reality and theory or research findings, it might assist my work.

In Atlanta, I was introduced to some of these young civil rights activists by M. Carl Holman, a professor at Clark College (who was later to head the National Urban Coalition). The youths conducted demonstrations like a military operation. Holman would get a call asking him to be at his phone at a specified time. The caller would not say why; Holman was trusted more than most older adults, but not entirely.

At the specified time, a caller would ask him to tell the police to come to a particular department store. Split-second timing was essential. If the police were alerted too early, they would prevent the demonstration. If they came too late, the youths might be roughed up by passers-by. At one demonstration I watched, the call was made by someone posted at a phone booth on federal property opposite the store. It was cold, so a stock of woolen ski caps was kept on hand for the demonstrators.

I was a Northern white—gently reared, I came to think—and wholly unprepared for the abuse and provocations tossed at these young people, particularly at the young women. How they kept their eyes straight ahead and refrained from reacting was beyond my understanding. However, it was borne in on me that a woman walking the picket line was only practicing the rigid discipline that had kept black girls alive and unmolested, if it did, walking the Main Streets of the Southern towns in which they grew up. It was not so different for the young men.

Many of these young people came from middle-class families; some did not. None seemed to rely on professors or parents for support. In general, their parents were made anxious by these activities and would try to dissuade them from participating. Then what did they have from their parents? They had been taught that they were equal, even though this assertion was frequently couched in ironic expressions like "All people are equal. Oh yeah!" Or, "We're all equal. It's just that some are more equal than others!"

It occurred to me that white people had been tuned into

(and were meant to be tuned into) the wry negation in these observations but that the affirmative message had been passed from generation to generation until, with relative safety, it could come alive. I concluded that the human spirit organizes personal resources believed absent, or instrumental to quite other purposes, when it is given a chance. I recalled this with the developments in Eastern Europe after 1989.

What did I take from the field trip for the purposes of my work? I was forever after skeptical of "culture of poverty" generalizations and such permutations as the concept of the "underclass."[12] Also, I realized that social science is in the business of disseminating and elaborating upon conventional attitudes rather than criticizing and correcting them. Social science seemed to me to be one kind of evidence, but never to be accepted uncritically.

While in Atlanta, I paid a courtesy call to a county welfare office. It was dark and dilapidated—one large room occupied by five or six black social workers and, now, me. I sat in a battered chair across the desk from the office supervisor, and she told me a little about their work. At one point, I asked to use the restroom and there was a sudden shifting of eyes. In Georgia at the time whites could not legally use black restrooms, and vice versa, and here there was no white restroom. Pressed, they let me use the black restroom. Then I understood a more personal problem: It humiliated them to let me see their miserable facilities.

The big push in welfare at the time (and in waves thereafter) was to encourage self-esteem in recipients. So I listened to the supervisor explain how they were building self-esteem in their clients while my gaze roamed around the room, like a camera panning, taking in the anguished black faces, the battered desks, the neglect and dirt. It was eerie, a conversation about self-esteem overlaid on every evidence of the contempt in which they—and their clients more than they—were held.

An experience like this did not so much alter my view of

social service, as confirm my conviction that there has to be a fit between what people are enjoined to do and the reality of their lives. To phrase this in educational terms, this is to say that students learn as much from how their professors behave as from what they teach. So I never failed to notice when the teaching of self-esteem and talk about empowerment coincided with budget cuts, and drives to train people for work coincided with high entry-level unemployment.

In the field, I also learned how segregation permeated the department's practices, despite its earnest, top-level commitment to desegregation. Black professionals in its regional offices were more scarce than officials in Washington seemed at all prepared to believe. I proposed a head count but Civil Service regulations forbade asking about race and, for a short while longer, the National Urban League opposed a change in these regulations.[13]

In the Southern states that they visited, black consultants from the U.S. Children's Bureau dealt only with black staff. A black senior consultant, Annie Lee Sandusky, explained to me, not without pain, that she was limited to the choice of helping black children in Southern states by dealing only with black staff or not helping them. She chose to help them. In the face of the sweeping movement for desegregation, these practices were not to survive much longer.

After publication of the "purple pamphlet," in 1962, I turned to the issue of housing for poor people. I had encountered housing problems in my earlier work. The family tensions of ADC recipients and Old Age Assistance recipients were exacerbated by the crowded, substandard housing that they occupied. Seeking solutions, I was told that housing came under the purview of the Housing and Home Finance Agency (HHFA). But HHFA seemed to think that, apart from the provision of public housing, meeting the needs of poor people belonged in HEW. This created a vacuum that one must abhor, and I undertook to fill it. I was taken in hand by W. C. ("Bud") Dutton, Jr., executive of the American Institute of Planners, and

Olive Swinney, a housing specialist in HEW's Bureau of Public Assistance. As always, I read widely, toured low-income housing sites and conferred with experts at universities.

I recall this work with great pleasure. The field is fascinating; it combines policy with architecture, city planning, sociology, financing and economics. In what had come to seem a natural sequence, I wrote a book called *Slums and Social Insecurity*.[14] The title was a disingenuous attempt to head off a question that would surely be asked: *Why would the Social Security Administration publish a book about housing?* In the end, the agency simply said that it was the first of a series of research reports dealing with broad aspects of economic and social security. It seemed, briefly, that HHFA might object to publication, but it did not—owing I believe to the intercession of Nathan Glazer, a distinguished sociologist, who in 1963 was a consultant to HHFA's administrator.

In all candor, I thought the book quite good. It demonstrated, to my satisfaction at least, that housing policies could help people escape poverty or help to keep them poor. In addition to government policies, it canvassed city planning, architectural and entrepreneurial practices as well, and outlined their consequences. It set forth specific recommendations, some of which dealt with the interrelationship of social security and housing policies (how public assistance payments should figure in payment for public housing, for example).

Discernible effects of the book were puzzling. It went through several reprintings; people in the field, especially at universities, were enthusiastic about it; and I received compliments on it as much as twenty years afterward. On the other hand, I never encountered a policy initiative that seemed to owe anything to the book's findings. Housing officials did not speak of it warmly—most did not speak of it at all. Probably they thought it academic, with or without dipping into it. Undoubtedly off-putting was the book's opening chapter, which reviewed relevant research.

Despite a succession of scholarly books and articles, it was not until years afterward that I set foot in a classroom as a proper teacher, nor did I think of myself as an academic. Indeed, when a friend, Karl de Schweinitz, suggested that I apply for a Fulbright grant, my instant response was, "I thought that was for professors."

Still, the idea was attractive and, after applying, I was awarded a Fulbright fellowship at the London School of Economics, where I extended my work on housing to British housing policy.[15] That was a rich year, 1962–63, intellectually and otherwise. Most rewarding of all was working with Richard M. Titmuss, chairman of the Department of Social Administration—a field he had invented. Titmuss was perhaps the only true genius I have known well—egalitarian, subtle, decent, a man who like so many English reformers lived privately by his public principles.

In the months before taking up the Fulbright, I was bent on using the insights into housing I had developed in some practical application of government policy, and 1962 was a good time to try. With President John F. Kennedy in office, new people in charge at HEW and HHFA, and a widespread sense that the government should and could contribute to solving social problems, there was a considerable wish to display what the government could accomplish. My idea was tailored to this wish. I proposed that we set up a joint task force of HEW and HHFA, select one or two public housing projects, and bring together at these sites all the considerable resources available to the government.

The two secretaries (Robert C. Weaver of HHFA and Abraham Ribicoff of HEW) liked the idea and approved the launching of a project called Concerted Services.[16] I shared chairmanship of the project's Joint Task Force with Abner Silverman, assistant commissioner of HHFA's Public Housing Administration. We convened representatives of all the agencies that might conceivably have something to offer, and chose the Pruitt Igoe

development in St. Louis—a large and troubled housing project, widely known because it had won prizes for architectural
design—as our first site.

Then and no doubt still, departments like HEW and HHFA
resembled the Commonwealth of Independent States rather
more than the Soviet Union. One could not, even in the name
of the secretary, simply order agencies to funnel resources to
the project. Agencies and their bureaus have their own procedures for allocating staff and money (many of these procedures
deriving from law, after all), and they have their own citizen
constituencies and ties to Congress, to which an administration
must be sensitive. So Silverman and I proceeded by sweet
reason, by persuasion, by bluff and by pressures directly and
indirectly applied. Among the pressures was the substantial
engagement in the project of the governor of Missouri and the
mayor of St. Louis. In the end, there was considerable investment of social services money, library money, juvenile delinquency money, money for research, public housing money and
housing demonstration grant money.

Nevertheless, the Pruitt Igoe Concerted Services Project
failed. The high-rise development was already in considerable
trouble when the project began. Crime, vandalism and rent
delinquency multiplied and the buildings deteriorated. After a
variety of efforts to salvage the situation, the government decided simply to move everyone and clear the land. Seared into
the memories of those who watched on television was the
implosion of these modernistic towers, an indelible but wholly
misleading symbol that public housing cannot work.

In retrospect, one could see that every possible mistake
had been made in planning Pruitt Igoe. The development was
set down in the midst of a large urban renewal area—attractive
because the land was available at no cost and without Not-In-
My-Backyard struggles; but the location meant that there were
no services (waste collection, for example), no shops and no jobs
nearby. Because it was an undesirable location, from the begin-

ning only the most troubled and stigmatized families would live in Pruitt Igoe.

Design efforts aimed at saving money created problems: There were no public toilets at ground level. Children and deliverymen urinated in the elevators which, perversely, were paneled with a material that combines with urine and deteriorates. Elevators stopped only at alternate floors, leaving tenants vulnerable to muggers on the flights of stairs they had to negotiate. As problems cycled—for example, desirable tenants, finding alternatives, moved out and those who remained were more uniformly troublesome—police became slow to answer calls. In the midst of all this chaos, HEW and HHFA were solemnly providing social workers, family life education, and training for teachers!

I learned an unwelcome lesson: Pathological physical and social arrangements and deficiencies in *basic* services cannot be compensated for by social services, no matter how skillful and well intended.

Having assimilated this lesson, I was not pleased when I found that the Community Service Society, to which I came as general director some twelve years later (see Chapter 7), was providing social services in a 1,400-unit housing rehabilitation project—the Diego-Beekman Project—in the South Bronx.[17] The housing project suffered from problems similar to Pruitt Igoe's. A major truck route ran through it, bringing noise, dirt and difficulty in controlling traffic. Crime was rampant and the police were unresponsive. Trash collection was poor.

In the interests of diversity, the proportion of welfare families was supposed to be limited. When no other families applied for apartments, however, the developers yielded to financial exigency. CSS was doing tenant selection (but in the circumstances, everyone who would come was taken anyway) and helping with tenant organization.

In terms of its stated objectives, the Diego-Beekman project failed. There were beneficiaries of the project, to be sure. As

Deep Throat is said to have advised a *Washington Post* reporter investigating Watergate: "Follow the money." When the federally subsidized developer took over what had been privately owned properties, one savings and loan association was able to retrieve its money from at least 28 properties on which it had foreclosed. Investors got profits on a base of $30 million for an investment of $5 million, plus a tax shelter. But the standard housing that was provided to poor people had a useful life of five or six years—no more.

However, this matter of Diego-Beekman came well after my assignment in the Social Security Administration. Except for this, the material in this chapter is a roughly sequential account of my work from 1958 to 1964. Work on child poverty and income maintenance was carried on throughout this period but soon took on a special direction. We now turn to this.

NOTES

1. Jacob Fisher, *Security Risk,* Piney Branch Press, Sarasota, Florida, 1986.

2. Alvin L. Schorr, *Explorations in Social Policy,* Basic Books, New York, 1968.

3. Alvin L. Schorr, "Problems in the ADC Program," *Social Work,* V, no. 2, April 1960.

4. W. L. Mitchell, Commissioner, memorandum to Miss Kathryn Goodwin, Director, Bureau of Public Assistance, 2 February 1960.

5. Schorr, "Problems in the ADC Program," op cit.

6. For example, see Orville Brim, *Education for Child Rearing,* Russell Sage Foundation, New York, 1959.

7. Social Scientists Advisory Meeting, "Summary of Deliberation," 20–21 June 1960. Mimeographed. U.S. Social Security Administration, Washington, D.C. Published as "Priorities in Family Life," *Papers in Social Welfare,* no. 3, Brandeis University, Waltham, Massachusetts.

8. Alvin L. Schorr, *Filial Responsibility in the Modern American Family,* U.S. Social Security Administration, U.S. Government Printing Office, Washington, D.C., 1960. An updated revision was published as *"Thy Father and Thy Mother," A Second Look at Filial Responsibility and Family Policy,* U.S. Social Security Administration, Washington, D.C., 1980.

9. Ibid.

10. Raymond Moley, "HEW Denies Children Have Duty to Parents," *Human Events*, XVII, no. 50, 15 December 1960, p. 637.

11. For contemporary statements about this, see Kurt W. Back, "Sociology Encounters the Southern Protest Movement for Desegregation," paper presented to the International Sociological Association, Washington, D.C., September 1962; and Everett C. Hughes, "Race Relations and the Sociological Imagination," paper presented to the American Sociological Association, Los Angeles, 28 August 1963.

12. Alvin L. Schorr, "The Nonculture of Poverty," *American Journal of Orthopsychiatry*, 34, no. 5, October 1964, pp. 907–12. See also "The Culture of Poverty," Agenda Paper for the White House Conference to Fulfill These Rights, 4 November 1965. Unpublished.

13. Letter from Whitney M. Young, Jr. (incoming director of the National Urban League) to Alvin L. Schorr, 29 May 1961; and letter from Lester B. Granger (outgoing director of the National Urban League) to Alvin L. Schorr, 29 June 1961.

14. Alvin L. Schorr, *Slums and Social Insecurity*, U.S. Government Printing Office, Washington, D.C., 1963.

15. Alvin L. Schorr, *Slums and Social Insecurity*, Thomas Nelson and Sons, London, 1964. A British edition, incorporating new material on British policy.

16. The terms secretary and department in these paragraphs are premature, strictly speaking. At the time, federal housing agencies were assembled in the Housing and Home Finance Agency, which was headed by an administrator, Robert Clifton Weaver. It became the Department of Housing and Urban Development in January 1966, when Weaver was named its first secretary. Secretary Abraham Ribicoff approved the Concerted Services Project for HEW, but chief responsibility lay with Wilbur J. Cohen, who was then assistant secretary for legislation at HEW. He became secretary in 1968.

17. "Diego-Beekman Housing Project, A Report on a Community Service Society Social Service Program in a Rehabilitated Housing Project in the South Bronx," Office of Program Planning and Research, Community Service Society, New York, September 1974. Unpublished.

Welfare:
A Spectator Sport

Two principles or convictions were solidified for me in my work at the Social Security Administration; they have guided my work since. One is that, in a country like the United States, poverty is a relative matter. The level of living that is regarded as minimally adequate is a social judgment about the relationship between minimal needs and what most people have. For reasons that no one seems quite to understand, the public's perception of minimal needs—the poverty level—is usually about half of median family income in the United States.[1] As real income rises, imperceptibly the public's definition of poverty floats upward.

One can observe this in the way legislators and analysts dealing with poverty have come, over the years, to focus on those living at 133 percent and then 185 and even 200 percent of the government's fixed poverty level.[2] These increments reflect ratcheting levels of dissatisfaction with the 1959 official poverty level, which has since been adjusted only in response to the cost of living.

The other principle, not unrelated, is that in the industrialized world it is not the low income level per se of the poorest portion of the population that promotes grievance. Rather, it is disparities in the *share* of national income among richer and poorer portions of the population.[3] In a why-to-do-it and how-to-do-it book in 1977, I set forth as a goal that the poorest 20 percent of the population should have at least 10 percent of national income.[4] (A 10 percent goal would make it theoretically possible for all low-income families to have at least half of median income.) A measure of the failure of that book to persuade is readily available: In 1980, the poorest 20 percent had 5.4 percent of national income; in 1990, they had 4.3 percent. One might say that the poorest 20 percent had lost 20 percent in "market share." It was not a good decade for my guideline.

At any rate, such convictions led me to cast a wide net in my preoccupation with poverty. I had to be concerned not just with welfare and narrowly defined poverty programs but with social security, taxation, social services, housing and virtually all government activities that distribute benefits. I tended to be critical of proposed new benefits for the poor if they appeared to be accorded in exchange for or as a distraction from new, much richer benefits for the wealthy. And I was interested in the situation of working-class people as well as the poor—in part because I do not think consequential sums of money can be "targeted" to "the truly needy" quite as sharply as became fashionable to believe.

Early in my work on ADC, I became convinced that re-forms dealing with the program alone were not likely to resolve its problems. ADC had been designed at a time when women were encouraged to stay at home and care for children. We were moving into a time when women—especially welfare recipi-ents—would be expected to work. The program had been designed for widowed mothers. Now, increasingly, it was serv-ing divorced, separated and unmarried mothers. My initial report on ADC said that the program was stigmatized and stigmatizing. As marital and employment trends matured, so-cial disfavor would only increase. In short, a program designed for one social climate was slipping into another, and would serve it poorly. The nation was bound to be at war with the program, and the program with its own conflicting objectives. Children and single parents required a more solid and widely approved institutional base for help.

Here was a dilemma. One could work on long-term solutions, but millions of women and children lived with

ADC in the short term. I could not fix my eyes on the horizon and gaze out above the distress—deepening distress, as the years went by—of current clientele. On the other hand, long-term solutions were going to be needed. I resolved the dilemma for myself, if this is a resolution, by working with both strands of the problem.

Sometimes I dealt with one strand and then with the other and sometimes with both simultaneously. In the material that follows, I will try to separate them, dealing with improving ADC in this chapter and with my efforts to find more suitable, long-term income programs in Chapter 5.

Separation of Cash Benefits and Services

In its early days, ADC was conceived of as a social work program. Its clients were in difficulty and vulnerable, and it seemed reasonable that the caseworker who authorized the payment of money should be able to offer counsel and guidance as well. Actually, few line workers were professionally trained social workers, but their supervisors and administrators were; and the program's ethos was rooted in social work. As Congress became restive about the program, inquiring in the 1950s into whether it fostered dependency, illegitimacy and juvenile delinquency, HEW and constituency groups argued that en-riched social services would reduce these problems. There-fore, in 1956 Congress amended the legislative statement of purposes to emphasize social services and, when that did not have much effect, in 1962 provided cash subsidies for social services.

An integrated program has its own problems, however. It is virtually impossible to regard the guidance given by social workers as separate from their decision to give cash assistance or not. In the mid-1960s there was considerable, justified criti-cism that legally entitled applicants were failing to receive assistance. Studies showed that fewer than half of those entitled to participate did so. Either they were reluctant to apply (but why?) or were improperly being denied. The civil rights and anti-poverty movements asserted rights and repudiated the paternalism implicit in social services. If cash benefits and services were administered separately and the application for cash benefits made a more or less clerical procedure, the question of entitlement (yes or no, period) should become simpler and more focused.

Moreover, a study based on reading case records in six cities showed that not much was actually being delivered to ADC recipients in the way of social services—despite integrated programs.[5] Statistical counts somewhat confused the matter because *any* face-to-face contact with an adult about a child (read: any contact at all concerning ADC) was counted as a social service. With separation, routine public assistance intevrviews could not masquerade as social services; they would have to be accounted for independently.

Political developments made a change comparatively easy to achieve. HEW Secretary John Gardner was reorganizing the department in order to rationalize programs which had been incorporated by accretion and to vest more overall control in his office. A proposed restructuring of public assistance would fit in nicely. Moreover, Congress was growing impatient, ultimately observing with a certain crispness that "those [social service amendments] have not had the results which those in the administration who sponsored the amendments predicted."[6] In other words, dependency, delinquency and illegitimacy were not being prevented or corrected by social services. Separating the administration of cash benefits and social services would not upset Congress.

In the fall of 1966, Assistant Secretary Lisle Carter and I consulted with the American Public Welfare Association and other constituency groups; the obligatory outside task force was constituted, and it delivered a recommendation in favor of separation.[7] Separation became a feature of HEW's reorganization in 1967 and, notwithstanding a transition from President

Lyndon Johnson to President Richard Nixon, in 1972 states were required to reorganize in similar fashion.

Much in social welfare policy fails to work as it would in an orderly world. Just as the HEW reorganization was being announced, Congress was perversely enacting strict requirements that ADC applicants should be assessed for employability and counseled with respect to employment. Congress also required states to make sure that recipients were counseled about family planning. In other words, while HEW was moving towards separation and routinizing procedures, Congress was moving toward more social services in welfare and more complex administration. There was some confusion.

A probably more serious complication was that the changeover occurred just as the welfare-rights movement was becoming most militant. Social workers who knew the clients or at least had experience were replaced by clerical workers, who were handicapped not so much by lack of professional training as by inexperience. Many of them were simply afraid of their clients. They dealt with their fear with various techniques of avoidance, such as not answering the telephone. It took some years for the workers who stayed into the 1970s to recover their equilibrium, and memory of those tense times no doubt colored the work they did thereafter.

To complicate matters further, many state welfare departments took the changeover as the moment to switch from caseloads to a so-called case bank system—a change not required by HEW. With a case bank, recipients do not have a single worker who is responsible for them. Rather, contacts are handled episodically by any worker who is available. At first glance, but only at first glance, this seems to improve efficiency. For a short time, it masked the fact that caseloads were growing beyond reason. Also, it made it unclear who was responsible for a particular client and distanced workers from the problems of the clients; perhaps these were ulterior motives for the change.

Thus, separation added to a deterioration of welfare administration that was already under way for a variety of reasons: rising caseloads, public obloquy, underfunding and downgrading of staff, sinking morale, intolerable rates of turnover, and a thinning out of administrators who had a sense of mission. Some thought that separation had caused the evident chaos and, by the early 1980s, a brisk discussion was under way about whether to reintegrate cash benefits and social services. In time, this discussion faded away, largely, I think, because the problems of welfare administration had become so overwhelming that separation came to seem a minor issue.

My own view is that separation is not better than integration in principle, or at all times. It is better or worse in the light of what we are trying to accomplish; and the overriding social need of the 1960s and 1970s (and the 1980s and early 1990s*) was to establish that law, not a worker's discretion, determines eligibility. Integration may work better when assistance is already clearly administered in accordance with law. In that circumstance an integrated program can, without compromising rights, more readily attend to the service needs of its clientele.

Mister, Miss, and Mrs.

In Chapter 3, I described a visit to a welfare office in Atlanta and observed how self-deluding talk of self-esteem may be. Now deputy assistant secretary at HEW, in 1967, I saw it a little differently. I joined a tour of anti-poverty programs in Mississippi. On a side trip, I visited a man who had filed suit against the State of Mississippi, charging that the state had not used due process in terminating his $50 a month disability grant.

---

*In enacting the Personal Responsibility and Work Opportunity Reconciliation Act of 1996, Congress and the president formally wiped out legal entitlement. State laws will now determine who may get assistance (but as charity, not as a right) and it will become a great deal more complicated to know whether law or equity is being observed.

I talked to Mr. Williams, standing up in his shack, a single room perhaps twelve feet square, with the fields outside visible through cracks between the wallboards. Four or five young children lay on beds that filled most of the room. Flies buzzed around us. Williams had lost one arm at the elbow and he had leukemia. He was visibly ill and was not likely to live long; his expression was dour. By then, I had been in Mississippi long enough to have an idea of the atmosphere of intimidation that black Mississippians felt, and I asked him where he got the guts to file suit against the state. A most thin smile creased his lips. "When I go to the welfare office now," he said, "they call me Mister."

This is how I learned that, in Mississippi, black welfare recipients were Mary or Joe or Willie but never Mister or Miss or Mrs. This was strictly contrary to federal regulations, of course. My general inclination had been to focus on who can get payments and at what levels of payment and to come to fine points of relationship later. Now I decided that if it was so important to Williams to be called Mister, it would be important to me, too. And so, for the months while I remained in government, I spent more time on this matter than I could well afford. Notwithstanding my lofty perch in the department, I did not succeed nor was this matter straightened out for ten years more. Evidently, this elementary courtesy had to wait for a new generation of welfare workers.

Entitlement and Level of Assistance

As I have indicated, many who were eligible for ADC did not apply or were rejected. As welfare rights activity heated up in the late 1960s, the proportion of presumably eligible people who received assistance improved, but then declined again as pressures on welfare departments grew worse. Average payment levels, never adequate, went into a steady fall from 1970 and had by 1995 declined, in real money, by almost half. Another statistic sums up these points more broadly: In 1979,

programs such as ADC removed 8 percent of all families with
children from poverty; by 1989 this figure had fallen to 5
percent.[8]

Over the years, many ideas have come together and become accepted as conventional wisdom that constrict the availability of welfare and serve to demean and harass those who
receive it. One such set of ideas produced increasingly draco-
nian requirements that recipients train for work and demonstrate that they are seeking work. From beginning to end, from
the Work Incentive amendments of 1967 to the Family Support
Act of 1988, in practice these programs failed again and again
in fundamental ways.

First, they were based on wholly erroneous ideas of
whether jobs would be available. ADC recipients have an
average reading level of sixth to eighth grade. With whatever
training may be provided, few will qualify for more than an
entry-level job. Taken job market by job market (because a
vacancy in Silicon Valley helps few welfare recipients in the rust
belt of Ohio), there are not nearly enough entry-level jobs to go
around. For example, a study of the Cleveland area found that
there would be "more than two applicants for every entry level
job opening in the region. Many recipients would either dis-
place other workers or be unable to find work. The competition
for scarce job openings in locations near recipients' homes
would be even more intense."[9]

Second, because of the educational deficits of the ADC
clientele, real training for work is a long and expensive process.
Even in the years before government deficits preoccupied us,
Congress and the states would not spend nearly as much for
training as is required. This left welfare departments and their
clients mindlessly observing empty, bureaucratic requirements. Women (mostly) received cursory training for work that
gave them no grip on such jobs as were, in fact, available.

Third, the target clientele was mothers. Especially as Congress required those with younger and younger children to

participate, mothers could not sign up unless day care was available. This necessary support suffered from the problem just noted—that is, that Congress and states did not provide the sums of money that florid speeches on the floors of Congress promised.

It is not as if legislators were simply insincere. Over twenty-five years, it was clearly established that even well-funded, competently conducted programs produce only marginal improvement in income for only some participants. Lack of basic education handicaps them and family emergencies—these are one-parent families—trip them up. This means that the government gains little or nothing financially for its considerable outlays. However legislators may have been forewarned, this is not what they expected. Subject to other pressures, in the end they do not provide necessary funding.

Finally, the organization of major job training and work efforts adds stress and complexity to the work of already vastly overtaxed welfare departments. That they do not function well is another reason these work and training programs turn out badly. To be sure, recipients are required to fetch and carry, to turn up and queue up, to document and demonstrate. When they miss a step along the way, they may be dropped from assistance. *There* is a cost savings, and a major reason that those entitled to aid failed to receive it.

In short, these are people with recalcitrant problems about working and there has never been enough government funding, never enough services, and at the end never enough jobs. Nor, if experience is an indication, will there be.

Congressional infatuation with welfare-to-work programs began to take shape in 1967. Frustrated with HEW's recommendations to rely on social services, the powerful chairman of the House Ways and Means Committee, Wilbur Mills, designed the first Work Incentive Program (dubbed WIN to avoid having it known as WIP). Mills collaborated closely with HEW's undersecretary, Wilbur Cohen. Formal comment on

such legislative proposals traveled from the commissioner of
Public Assistance to me (then deputy assistant secretary) and
then to Cohen.[10] I wrote memoranda to him expressing opposition to the legislation and, so strongly did I feel about this,
resorted to the (to me) alien bureaucratic maneuver of burying
the formal documents in my "in" basket. One late afternoon
was punctuated by the appearance of Cohen's secretary, cool
and dignified, saying that she was sent to find the documents
in my office if I could not. I could sign them or not, as I pleased.

There was widespread external opposition to WIN, generally for the reasons I have outlined, but nothing availed. The
WIN amendments were attached to the Social Security Amendments of 1967, which passed. It should be recorded that, in the
outcome, they were "judged inadequate for not delivering on
the promise of change."[11]

I was incensed, thinking the department's support of the
legislation an abandonment of people we were supposed to
serve and protect. The Social Security Amendments of 1967
provided increases for social security beneficiaries and so were
as nearly veto-proof as may be. Nevertheless, I set out to call
around the country, organizing a campaign to persuade the
president to veto the bill. It was the only time in my career that
I used my position for flat-out opposition to departmental
policy.

Probably, I thought about a conversation with Wilbur
Cohen earlier that year. Considering whether to accept appointment as deputy assistant secretary at HEW, I had asked him
what my position would be if I felt obliged to speak out in
opposition to department policy. He thought for a moment and
said, "You had better be right!"

President Lyndon Johnson did not veto the bill, of course,
and I drew no reaction at all from any of the people who might
have taken me to task. Only, shortly afterward, while I was
going through a receiving line at a White House reception,
Lyndon Johnson looked quizzical and asked me what I took to

be a rhetorical question: "What was *that* about?" He seemed so weary and troubled that my only emotion was to feel sorry for him.

I entertained the idea of resigning over the issue, and asked for an appointment with the secretary, John Gardner. On one hand was a question of principle and, on the other hand, much might yet be accomplished if I stayed. Gardner gave no advice. It was, he said thoughtfully, "a classical dilemma." This response took on a certain poignancy when, a couple of weeks later, he resigned himself. The issue, it was said, was budget allocations for social programs.

The March on Washington

I was not sorry to have stayed at HEW. It was a time of great danger and large challenges. Following the Detroit conflagrations and riots in July 1967, many senior government officials went through what seemed to me a period that was akin to clinical depression. In judgment they seemed unaffected, but they did not show their accustomed energy and seemed, in one way and another, to be adjusting to a sense of loss. The radical fringe and apocalypticists had been warning that our house was on fire; once again, the metaphor turned into reality. Because Detroit was a showplace city of the War Against Poverty, the insult was double. The loss suffered by those government officials may have been their sense of innocence—their conviction (*our* conviction) that earnest intentions and exhausting activity would prevent or, at least, retard events.

One day in 1968, I stood at an office window and looked out at the pall of smoke that rose from near-northwest Washington burning—the fury in the ghettoes now brought home to the nation's capital. I have not since seen smoke from a burning building without sensing its acrid taste and thinking of that time.

That very day, the HEW building was closed because of a bomb threat. My secretary, Winonah Warren, a black woman, was married to a white man. He called to tell her to wait for him to take her home. She smiled ruefully and explained, "He's coming to protect me, but he needs *me* to protect *him*." Most upsetting of all was the flood of radio call-in comments as I drove home: "Kill the niggers," "Hunt them down." I felt poised between numbness and despair.

Martin Luther King, Jr. had been assassinated earlier that year and the ghettoes of the nation bristled with pain and with anger. The Southern Christian Leadership Conference had planned a March on Washington and, in the wake of King's assassination, determined to carry it out. They came to Washington and camped between the White House and the Potomac, on fields that a steady rain turned into mud. From day to day, they proceeded up Independence Avenue, calling on government departments in sequence, presenting demands and conducting negotiations on behalf of the poor and disadvantaged.

Wilbur Cohen, now HEW secretary, asked me to organize a departmental response to the Poor People's March. There were two moods in the government. One was anxious and militant; large demonstrations at the seat of power invariably produce a tightly defensive reaction. The other reaction, which seemed to proceed from the president and Attorney General Ramsey Clark, was that the demonstrators were our people, that they were deeply hurt, and that we had to show that we cared for them.

Many HEW employees, a group of "Young Turks" in particular, set out voluntarily to help the people in what became known as Resurrection City, delivering food, blankets and other necessities. Encouraged by my assistant, Nancy Amidei, they spent time talking to the marchers. Formally, I instructed the department's agencies to review their programs, considering grievances and likely demands, and to submit a roster of program improvements that could and should be made.

The confrontation with HEW, when it came, proved to be civil. Security officers were near at hand though out of sight, but there was no disturbance. The marchers were invited into the department's auditorium, where a number of assistant secretaries waited to listen to them. The marchers declined to talk to anyone except the secretary. While they waited for Cohen to arrive, the "Children of the Universe" sang. One song began:

> Tired of drinking from a ghetto cup,
> Don't give a damn,
> Ain't gonna give up.
> Do right, white man,
> Do right,
> Before I get mad . . .
> Before I get mad.

One of the Children, Jimmy Metcalf, talked for a few minutes. "Oh, we gonna change things," he said. "Yes, sir. Things are going to be different. Our folks aren't going to be sad, either, they're not going to be sad they brought us into a lousy world— 'cause it ain't gonna be lousy and they're gonna be proud."

Concluding that he should attend, Wilbur Cohen walked down the aisle of the auditorium with characteristic aplomb, accompanied hand in hand by a child who happened to be standing at the entrance. Speakers addressed their demands to him; one spoke Spanish, which he then patronizingly translated into English. When Cohen responded in Spanish and English, he seemed to have won the crowd.

Over a period of several days, we acceded to a number of demands; others would require legislation; still others we thought improper or impractical. An issue to which I would be returning some years later concerned the date on which ADC payments begin. After entitlement is established in social security, payment is made retroactive to the first day of the month in which application was made. It was not so in ADC, and I had long thought this unfair. In most states, payment did not begin until the welfare department established eligibility (in some cases even later), so delay and confusion saved money for the government. Poor People's representatives demanded and the department agreed that this injustice should be corrected. Technicians began the process of writing a new regulation. By the time it was ready, however, Richard Nixon was president and the regulation was scrapped.

Outside the Government, Still Working on Welfare

Two administrations later, within days of assuming office in 1977, Secretary of HEW Joseph A. Califano, Jr. wrote to a number of people inviting advice on how to proceed with welfare reform. He was interested in broad proposals for reform, as well as discrete, constructive steps that might be taken by administrative action, that is, expeditiously. Now at the Community Service Society of New York (see Chapter 7), I responded that many of the officials who had promised retroactive payment for ADC were once more in the administration—Califano had himself been in charge of domestic policy in the Johnson White House—and were now in a position to deliver on the promise.

HEW studied the matter for two years, during which time I lobbied officials extensively; others did, too, of course. I called Marian Edelman—head of the Children's Defense Fund, who was influential with Califano—to ask if she would write him a letter that would be worth $100 million; and I believe that she did. Eventually, senior officials unanimously recommended that the change be made. Meanwhile, estimates of the additional cost had been prepared; they ranged upwards from $80 million a year. It was not a trivial sum and the Carter administration was facing a budget crisis. From the clients' point of view, of course, the sum indicated how much they were being cheated.

Califano wrote to me, saying that "due to budget constraints" he had to postpone making the policy change but would pursue the matter later. The change was never made. Aroused, I undertook to write a column for the *Washington Post* entitled "Ten Years Later, Another Promise Is Broken." The editor to whom I proposed the piece, Noel Epstein, said, "Okay, Alvin, but only if you wait a couple of weeks to write it." When I asked why he said, irrefutably, "because irony is better than indignation."[12]

I had left the government at the beginning of 1969, and continued to pursue ways to promote strictly proper determination of eligibility for assistance, broadened eligibility, decent levels of payment—an objective that grew more remote as the years went by—and simplified, efficient and courteous administration of the ADC program.

I testified before congressional committees; consulted with welfare departments—in New York City, in particular, where administrators Mitchell Ginsberg and James Dumpson were my friends and had been allies on many issues; lectured and wrote op-ed pieces, articles and books; lobbied congressmen and -women and drafted legislation; and devised creative ways to dramatize the issues for a wrongheadedly indoctrinated public.

For the U.S. Senate's "Hunger Committee" in 1970, I conducted a study of cash and food programs in Virginia. With the assistance of Carl Wagner, I looked into the interaction of public assistance with food stamps and other food programs to determine whether there was still a shortfall in meeting nutritional needs. There was.

Unexpectedly we also found problems of discrimination. Virtually everyone believed, and going in we believed, that white people living in the hills of Virginia were too proud to ask for help and so it was chiefly blacks who received welfare. However, careful reading of case records and statistical analysis made it clear that, no matter how proud, whites did apply for assistance; it was blacks who were underrepresented in the caseload. Rural and small-town welfare officials, operating in a paternalistic manner that was probably carried over from the nineteenth century, simply told blacks that they could manage somehow (*Get work, Mabel!*) and denied them assistance.

As was my practice, I showed a draft of our report to officials who might point out errors. One was HEW's regional director in Charlottesville, whom I had known for some time. He startled me by observing that this was all "old stuff" to him. "Why didn't you tell us?" I asked. "Why didn't you tell the secretary?" He answered with a sophisticated question: "Would he have wanted to know?"

The secretary had plenty of problems, as it was. A civil rights issue with a politically powerful, Democratic state was not what he needed. However, the incident illustrated a common problem in government: the shielding of senior officials by well-meaning aides. It may have been wrong to assume that the secretary would not have wanted to know. In any event, it *was* wrong to decide this for him.

The report went to the Senate committee and a copy to HEW, where enforcement, if it was undertaken, would trace a tortuous course from Washington to Charlottesville to Richmond to the various small towns at issue. The finding about discrimination provides one more illustration of a dynamic that operates to deny assistance to entitled people, perhaps especially in smaller population centers. That is, at each transfer point, the clarity and force of federal policy suffers more erosion.

The combination of inflation with recession after 1973 created particular dangers for welfare clients and the poor in general. Welfare caseloads could be expected to press upwards while inflation degraded the value of grants that were being provided. Starved for revenue, states would cut back on welfare in whatever ways they could find. In 1975, staff of the Community Service Society, working with the Center for Community Change in Washington, developed a "welfare cost stabilization program." This was designed to provide federal money to meet state costs if they would refrain from cutting back on eligibility and adjust grants to the cost of living. We could not sell the idea to Congress.

Somewhat before its time, a provision was included that would decouple Medicaid from welfare. States were required to certify all welfare recipients for Medicaid, but Medicaid cost them a great deal more than ADC. It was apparent that they would cut back on welfare primarily in order to save Medicaid money. We floated the idea that Congress should permit lower income eligibility levels for Medicaid than for ADC. The idea was shocking—it *is* shocking, but indeed states did bring down ADC income eligibility levels even faster than they would otherwise have done in order to save Medicaid money.

Improper Denials   At about the same time, the Community Service Society opened an office in Spanish (East) Harlem that might, in retrospect, be viewed as an early and spectacular experiment with privatizing public welfare. We announced that families who thought they had been denied welfare improperly might come to us for help. If we judged that they were strictly eligible, we would help them to establish the fact. While we were doing so, *CSS would provide the assistance* they should have been receiving.

The project carried a considerable cost. I tried to persuade my friend, Human Resources administrator James Dumpson, that eventually CSS should be reimbursed by the city, arguing that we were only spending money that HRA should have been spending. Unfortunately, neither friendship nor guilt extended so far. In rapid order we found scores of entitled applicants who had been turned down; the proof that they were eligible came when, on appeal, they were accorded assistance.[13] This led HRA to do its own sample review, and the *New York Times* reported that, of applications rejected at four of its offices in January 1978, 51 percent! had been denied improperly.[14]

Later, as a professor at Case Western Reserve University (CWRU) in 1981, I was involved in a somewhat similar project.[15]

We established field offices in cities in five Midwestern states
that offered legal and social work help (but no financial support) to families that had been denied assistance improperly.
Intended as a three-year project, it was ended in less than a year
because the federal agency that financed it, the Community
Services Agency (earlier the Office of Economic Opportunity),
was wiped out by Congress. Nevertheless, the project established that 150 families had been denied assistance improperly,
in violation of a wide variety of laws and regulations. One
welfare office limited the number of applications it would
accept. Another declined to accept applications from women
younger than eighteen, persisting in its refusal even after lawyers pointed out its illegality. A third office rejected an application because a prior employer in another state failed to submit
a statement about the applicant's employment.

It was distressing to learn that the kinds of help the CWRU
project offered were not readily available in each city. Social
service agencies seemed not to want to deal with the eligibility
issue. Possibly, welfare regulations had grown so complex that
voluntary agencies did not understand them. Possibly, they did
not want to offend the welfare department, which provided
many of them with funds for one project or another. Possibly,
their formal function did not include the assurance of basic
maintenance for families. In any event, the net result was that
the administration of welfare departments had become increasingly inimical to its clientele. With the exception of some badly
overburdened legal services programs, no one challenged
welfare departments to do what might be called consumer-
oriented monitoring.

Such conclusions earned headlines in one newspaper and
another and quickly slipped out of general consciousness. Welfare agencies did not alter their practices, nor was anyone
disciplined. There was not a sense of shock or indignation such
as might have accompanied the disclosure that insurance companies were failing to pay claims properly. The public's sense

of fair play had shifted somehow; people did not care or, perhaps, thought that this was merely one more example of poorly functioning public bureaucracy. *So what else is new!* and *what is there to do anyway!* Very likely, the departments themselves did not know how to correct the problem nor did they have the necessary energy.

Churning   The problem with applications for welfare is related to a problem that has come to be known in the business as "churning." That is, cases are terminated only to have the former recipients reapply within a month or two and demonstrate eligibility.[16] It is a good guess that such people have been eligible all the time and that someone—either the recipient or the worker—has made an error. From time to time, I analyzed welfare statistics in order to demonstrate the problem to administrators and elected officials. No one displayed sustained interest, let alone a determination to take corrective steps. When it comes to welfare, apparently, laws are observed only under pressure and then only with respect to specific instances.

A Spectator Sport

In my time at HEW, I thought that more constructive policies might be developed if only the public could be educated about the circumstances of recipients and the challenges in designing an effective and fair program for them. At one point I set out to draft a speech about public assistance for President Johnson. I was encouraged in this effort by the White House and even, at one point, was asked to find an appropriate university where he might use it as a commencement address.

The speech was not to be given; as intent as Lyndon Johnson was on improving the lives of poor people, he was uncomfortable with welfare, and it was unlikely from the beginning that he would address the subject. Nor, in 1968, was it easy for the president to speak publicly without provoking an anti-war demonstration.

However—and I digress—my effort led to a curious

luncheon with two presidential aides at a hotel near the White House. They said that they wanted to discuss welfare; yet there was very little discussion of welfare. The conversation seemed very general. What was the mood in the country? *Between riots in the ghettoes and demonstrations by the peace movement, not great.* What did I think of Hubert Humphrey? Would I campaign for him to succeed Lyndon Johnson? *I didn't know. I had thought of him as a great man, but his support of the war in Vietnam and his one-sided criticism of the student demonstrations during the August 1968 Democratic Convention in Chicago really disappointed me.* And so on.

Deciding to walk back to my office rather than take a taxi, I reflected that I had just tossed away my chance to become assistant secretary. Lisle Carter had resigned, I was acting assistant secretary and, in the closing months of a president's administration, it is simplest and not uncommon to fill these positions by promotion. A test was constructed and I failed it. Yet I *was* angry with Hubert Humphrey, though in no doubt about his considerable superiority to Richard Nixon. I had no way to establish that the conclusion I drew about the luncheon was correct, of course, and I did not spend much time thinking about it. There was not time. End of digression.

Where was I? I was introducing the notion of welfare policy as a spectator sport.

Over the last thirty-five years, public attitudes toward welfare recipients have shifted from vague hostility to deep hostility to deep and deeply ingrained hostility. For a long time, thinking that this shift must be a product of poor information, I looked for ways to engage the public with facts. However, welfare has been discussed without pause for years now and attitudes are far worse and worse informed than ever. For example, it is thought that couples separate in order to get welfare. This may happen here and there, but it is not a common pattern, as economists like Heather Ross and Isabel Sawhill— no soft-headed bleeding hearts, they—quite early pointed out.[17] So I wrote and spoke about the evidence, yet waited fearfully, as one waits in a cemetery for the midnight tolling of church bells, for each president in turn to complain from his bully pulpit about the incentive for couples to split up. None who has completed his term has so far disappointed me, and each has had a larger audience than I.

From time to time, HEW and advocacy groups such as the Children's Defense Fund published brochures with titles like "Myths About AFDC," documenting the fact that families do not stay on the program forever, that welfare dependency is not passed from one generation to the next, that the majority of recipients are white, that payments (including food stamps, Medicaid, and all the rest) are well below subsistence requirements, and so forth. The capacity of such information to penetrate the public's consciousness seems scant. One has to ask why.

It goes without saying that the past ten or fifteen years saw the rise of conservatism, for whose proponents welfare was a fat and time-honored target. But this does not explain the appearance of increasing viciousness toward welfare recipients, as if a vendetta were under way. I give but one example: For many years ADC provided no assistance to women pregnant with their first child. This seemed illogical. Depriving a pregnant woman produces a low birth-weight baby, with all the public costs that places on the health care system. So the program was amended to include such women—if they were otherwise qualified.

In 1981, AFDC was amended again to forbid payments during the first six months of such a pregnancy. It had occurred to someone that women might get pregnant deliberately in order to receive AFDC and then would abort, thus cheating the government. The secretary of the Department of Health and Human Services (the successor to HEW) estimated that $1 million—in a $10 billion program—would be saved by the change. That is, disqualification would rule out perhaps three hundred women. Of these, how many—one-third? one-tenth? none?—would have gotten pregnant in order to abort and cheat the government? Does it not seem peculiarly petty and mean (if not, indeed, paranoid) for the House Ways and Means Committee, which deals with all social security and tax legislation, to have occupied itself for even five minutes with this $1 million matter?

This kind of behavior contributed to my view, formed over a long time, that to most people welfare policy is not a set of practical issues that affects the lives of real people. It is a symbol, a myth, and a game.

For local, state, and federal legislators, welfare policy has been a symbol that they are prudent, businesslike, Calvinist (whatever their actual religion), and at one with their constituency. I have talked to some very impressive legislators—in opposing the 1988 redrafting of welfare legislation, for example—and have seen them persuaded in some measure by my arguments. When they asked and I advised them to seek instead some modest improvement in payment levels or some simplification of welfare regulations, it was plain that they were trapped by the politics of the matter. They could not fail to say they want to reform the behavior of the people in the system. They could not be seen to oppose the 1988 Family Support Act which Senator Daniel Patrick Moynihan, for one, described as "the moment we've waited for for half a century." (These moments are not always easily recognized; it is good to have them pointed out.)

Of course, legislators are, or would say that they are, responsible to their constituencies; and for their constituencies welfare is a myth. A myth is a set of ideas and memories of unknown origin that usually contains episodes and pronouncements that explain and support practices and attitudes that might otherwise seem inexplicable. Two factors in particular have fed this welfare myth.

First is the rising frustration and resentment among people who feel that for various reasons they have lost or are losing status, and who seek a scapegoat. Many people have lost status in these last twenty years. Despite my discussion of "the scapegoat phenomenon" in my first report on ADC, I had no premonition that the problem would come to loom so large. On the other side of the status ledger, the myth reinforces feelings of worth and worthiness among the financially successful. It is painful to reflect that successful people seek such support for their self-regard.

And, second, scapegoating welfare has served the purposes of political candidates; economists and other professionals, not limited to conservative professionals; government officials; business leaders; and others promoting agendas having to do with shrinking public expenditure—establishing that they are thinking freshly about policy, and promoting their own programs by counterposing them to welfare. Because welfare is a myth, it is not necessary to learn very much about it. If you say that recipients have to show a sense of responsibility to society (Are pensioners required to show a sense of responsibility to society? farmers receiving subsidies?) . . . if you say that recipients need new incentives or they will not work . . . if you say that recipients have babies to get welfare, you will not be challenged. One is spared the tedium of fact-finding.

Welfare policy has become a game; there is no entrance fee to play; everyone plays except the puck. It is a spectator sport. Playing or watching the welfare game is one of the few remaining celebrations of community that the rest of us have.

And so, though I do not desist (it is not in me to desist), I do not place much confidence in the broadening and enlightening influence of information and research in this field. I do not argue with taxi drivers, anymore. I come around again to the view that we need a different kind of institutional base for the needy, for women and young children in particular. In the next chapter, I describe some of my experiences in trying to promote such ideas.

NOTES

1. For a fuller explanation of the reasoning here, see Alvin L. Schorr, *Common Decency: Domestic Policies After Reagan,* Yale University Press, New Haven, Connecticut, 1986, Chapter 2. Two important references thirteen years apart, are Victor Fuchs, "Redefining Poverty," *The Public Interest,* no. 8, Summer 1967, p. 89; and Harold W. Watts, "Special Panel Suggests Changes in BLS Family Budget Program," *Monthly Labor Review,* December 1980.

2. For example, in 1989, two million families lived in states providing Medicaid to families with incomes between 133 and 185 percent of the poverty level, and 3.2 million to families over 185 percent of the poverty level. Participants in the Special Supplemental Food Program for Women, Infants, and Children had to have income below 185 percent of the poverty level. *Overview of Entitlement Programs,* House of Representatives, Committee on Ways and Means, 7 May 1991.

3. Harold L. Wilensky and Charles N. Lebeaux, *Industrial Society and Social Welfare,* 2d ed., Free Press, New York, 1965. Also, W.G. Runciman, *Relative Deprivation and Social Justice,* Routledge and Kegan Paul, London, 1966.

4. Alvin L. Schorr, ed., *Jubilee for Our Times: A Practical Program for Income Equality,* Columbia University Press, New York, 1977.

5. Bureau of Public Assistance, U.S. Department of Health, Education and Welfare, Washington, D.C., 1966. Unpublished. More generally, a history of public assistance observes: "The result [of 1956 social service legislation] was brief euphoria in social work ranks, but no appreciable change in state and local practice." Blanche Coll, *Safety Net: Welfare and Social Security, 1929–1979.* Rutgers University Press, New Brunswick, New Jersey, 1995.

6. *Report of the Committee on Ways and Means on H.R. 12080, Social Security Amendments of 1967,* 7 August 1967, Government Printing Office, Washington, D.C., 1967, p. 96.

7. *Task Force on Social Services,* Report to Assistant Secretary Lisle C. Carter, Jr., 1 September 1966. Also, in Martha Derthick, *Uncontrollable Spending for Social Services Grants,* The Brookings Institution, Washington, D.C., 1975, see Chapter 3, footnote 5.

8. Isabel V. Sawhill, "Perspectives," *Social Insurance Update No. 25,* National Academy of Social Insurance, Washington, D.C., September 1992.

9. Claudia V. Coulton, Nandita Verma and Shenyang Guo, with the assistance of Carmen Griffey and Edward Wang, "Time Limited Welfare and the Employment Prospects of AFDC Recipients in Cuyahoga County," Center on Urban Policy and Social Change, Case Western Reserve Uni-

versity, Cleveland, 11 October 1996. Processed. For a brief, circumstantial account of how difficult it is for AFDC mothers to get work, even when it looks relatively easy from a distance, see Katherine S. Newman, "What Inner-City Jobs for Welfare Moms?", *New York Times,* 20 May 1995, op-ed page.

10. For the source of Wilbur Cohen's views of welfare-to-work programs, see Edward D. Berkowitz, *Mr. Social Security: The Life of Wilbur J. Cohen,* University Press of Kansas, Lawrence, 1995, pp. 106–13 and 145–53. These pages also set forth his break with Arthur Altmeyer, head of the social security program from 1937 to 1953 and Cohen's close friend and mentor, over this matter: "Altmeyer deplored the practice of 'workfare.' "

11. Judith M. Gueron and Edward Pauly with Cameran M. Lougy, *From Welfare to Work,* Manpower Demonstration Research Corp., New York and San Francisco, 1991, p. 8.

12. Alvin L. Schorr, "Ten Years Later, Another Promise Is Broken," *Washington Post,* 18 March 1979.

13. Daniel Reich, "The Needy Get Iciness," *New York Times,* 29 September 1977.

14. Peter Kihss, "Half of H.R.A.'s Welfare Rejections Are Found Incorrect in Sampling," *New York Times,* 19 April 1978.

15. Marie Vesely with Sheila McEntee and Alvin L. Schorr, *Fair Play,* Mandel School of Applied Social Sciences, Case Western Reserve University, Cleveland, 1982.

16. An early publication on this matter was Peter Jordan and Alan Matthews, Barry Bluestone, Mario Fortuna, and Pam Megna, *Corrective Action and AFDC Dynamics: An Empirical Study in Six Jurisdictions,* Social Welfare Research Institute, Boston College, Boston, 1980.

17. Heather I. Ross and Isabel V. Sawhill, *Time of Transition,* The Urban Institute, Washington, D.C., 1975.

Quest for Reform

My search for a sounder institutional base for income support led to what I call mainstream solutions. *Mainstream* programs are not means tested, whatever other criteria for eligibility they may have. That is, eligibility may rest on age, or veteran status, or college attendance, or any other qualitative criterion, but does not require a demonstration that one has less than a specified amount of income.

For example, social insurance, which dominated income support programming in the United States from perhaps 1935 to the 1960s, is mainstream in principle. The government identifies major risks to income—old age, disability, widowhood, orphanhood, unemployment—and frames programs that guard against each risk. At no point in qualifying for any of these programs does one present evidence of poverty.

Mainstreaming has been criticized vigorously in the Western world since the mid-1960s, when a feeling that welfare state spending was getting out of hand began to grow. Means testing was seen as a way to limit spending, at least on the poor. Paradoxically, some argued simultaneously that means testing would assure *more* money for the poor because funds would not be wasted on recipients who were not poor. This argument, framed during the early raptures of cost-benefit analysts, seemed sincere if ingenuous.

The importance of mainstream solutions became clear to me when I observed the scapegoating of means-tested beneficiaries. Something there is in Americans that doesn't love a mendicant. Also, the nature of our political process makes it inevitable that, when government money is parceled out, programs with the least powerful constituencies will do worst. By definition, means testing assembles a politically weak constituency. However compassionate a means-tested program may be at initiation, in time the dynamics of interest-group politics degrades it.

Very early, it seemed to me that powerful forces polarize our citizenry—pitting the poor against the not so poor, whites against non-whites, the young against the elderly. The way income support has been structured is one such force. One has only to compare a welfare with a social security office or a public with a private medical clinic or a public with a private housing development to see how badly means-tested consumers are treated. Though I did not foresee how severe polarization was to become, I was searching for formulations that would serve people across lines of class and color.

One might think that polarization would lead to demonstrations and even violence by the underprivileged. So I have been baffled to observe the absence of activism among profoundly deprived people who are badgered and denied benefits to which they are entitled, or when benefits are reduced to intolerable levels. When the poor were reeling from the Reagan administration's "new and revised" War on Poverty in 1982, I had the opportunity to ask James Baldwin—the famous author and civil rights leader—to account for the absence of visible reaction. He had just returned to France, where he was living, from a tour of our Southern states to catch up on developments. "There *will* be a reaction," he predicted delphically, "but it will be different next time." Well, we shall see.

I would like not to be misunderstood. I do not wish for unrest—on the contrary, I passionately seek civility—but the passivity and despair that the absence of serious protest in the last twenty years represents is not civility. It is itself cause for anguish and alarm.

So I sought mainstream solutions because their political

dynamics would augur better things for disadvantaged people and because such solutions would tend to develop institutions that would promote cohesion rather than division. Two such solutions proved to be children's allowances and social security; the negative income tax that occupied national debate in the 1970s was, to my view, not a mainstream solution.

Children's Allowances

During my time at the Social Security Administration, I became interested in family or children's allowances. The children's allowance is a government payment to parents for each of their children. There is no test of means. In no country is the allowance enough to support a child, but it helps; as Europeans say, it "equalizes" the burden for families of different size.

Children's allowances had spread across Europe early in this century and been considerably enriched after World War II, when they were introduced in Canada. When doing research in France for the Social Security Administration, it struck me that French officials did not—as any American official would—identify large families or one-parent families as being particularly at risk of being poor. Their generous program of children's allowances seemed to account for this.[1]

Why had we not developed such a program in the 1940s or 1950s, when the rest of the Western world was doing so, or in the 1960s, when we were favored with the "fiscal dividend"? I thought there were three reasons. In Europe, children's allowances originated with employers as a strategy to depress wages. Large families received a supplement to their subsistence wages, thus alleviating their problem without requiring a general wage increase. Naturally, trade unions opposed this subsidy. In the end, when the unions won general wage increases anyway, children's allowances flourished to serve other purposes—now with the vigorous support of European trade unions. American trade unions assimilated the initial European hostility to children's allowances but were not paying attention when the European unions changed position. When, in the 1960s, American unions were finally prepared to adopt a supportive position, it was too late.

Second, in Europe children's allowances were long regarded as a device for raising the birth rate. In France, this view was embodied in a country saying, "Let's make a baby to buy a motorbike"; and in Paris in a fictional autobiography, which begins: "I was born of Allowances and a Holiday, of which the morning stretched out happily to the sound of 'I love you—You love me' played on a sweet trumpet."[2]

In the European experience with children's allowances after 1930, it became clear that such subsidies are not why babies get made. However, the public perception that these programs would raise the birth rate was unshaken. When government programs were expanding in the United States in the 1960s, the country was preoccupied with a population explosion; we were not going to do anything that one might think would add to the problem.

A third reason that we did not develop children's allowances when other countries did was that it was widely believed that children's allowances would be a Catholic measure. Although they did not press the point, Catholic leaders did in fact favor children's allowances. As American politics went until the 1950s, this greatly undermined chances of enactment.

Thus, I concluded that the reasons that a program of children's allowances had not developed in the United States rested on ideas that were refutable or on historical circumstances that had changed. Such ideas might no longer be persuasive.

The idea of developing children's allowances in the United States came up in the very first meeting of social scientist advisers that we had assembled in 1960.[3] But I was occupied with ADC and determined not to be perceived as criticizing ADC in order to advocate some favorite alternative. I delayed looking into children's allowances, but from that time the program was on my agenda.

Obviously, the view that children's allowances would raise the birth rate, particularly among poor people and blacks, would be fatal to the chances of such a program. In the hope of beginning a conversation in the United States that would counter this type of folklore, the Social Security Administration assembled a group of distinguished demographers.[4] They were asked to address the question of the relationship between income maintenance and the birth rate, overall and in special groups. Surveying various kinds of evidence—drastic efforts to raise birth rates in France, Germany and Italy; national experiences with children's allowances and welfare; and experience with American birth rates—the conferees concluded that a new income maintenance program would have little or no effect. In my own subsequent review, I said:

> The birth rate is compounded of income and one's conception of income, of education and ignorance, of conviction and faith, of geography and technology, of love and covetousness, of accident and design. . . . In all probability, a new income maintenance program would lead some people, including some who are poor, to have additional children. But this effect would be trivial in relation to concurrent developments and would not be discernible in subsequent population figures.[5]

In time, such ideas did in fact get spread around.[6]

Bridging my times at the Social Security Administration and the Office of Economic Opportunity in 1964 and 1965, I worked on a book about children in poverty called *Poor Kids*. I recall that my editor at Basic Books, Irving Kristol, winced at my desire to include photographs of poor children—he thought this sentimental—but the text was austere and pleased him. The book set forth statistics about poor children and the circumstances that led to their poverty and discussed a number of issues concerned with providing support for them: the effect on birth rates and work incentive and when support might lead to "take-off." As to this last question, I argued, paraphrasing W. W. Rostow's work on underdeveloped countries, that "take-off for poor families requires surplus money for self-improvement, as well as the skill and drive more usually asked of them."[7]

I outlined and discussed three alternative income maintenance programs, conscientiously structuring them in a fashion that: 1) would give the most money to poor families at the lowest overall cost; 2) would be most likely to promote "take-off"; 3) would be mainstream or at least resemble mainstream programs; 4) could readily be administered; 5) would not dampen incentive to work or create other undesirable consequences; and 6) would have an acceptable cost—no more than $2 or $3 billion a year.

The alternative programs I examined were a children's negative income tax, children's allowances, and a program called fatherless child insurance.*

The book had an excellent critical reception. Some of the ideas in it were new and, just as the War Against Poverty was taking shape, it brought information about childhood poverty together with ideas about how to mitigate it. In a review that began ominously: "The title and the touching pictures notwithstanding . . .," *The Economist* went on to say that the book displayed "formidable" expertise and interesting ideas.[10] It was

---

*Like other social insurances, fatherless child insurance (FCI) protects against a common risk, that is, the risk that a child's parents will divorce. Children whose parents have been subject to the social security payroll tax would receive benefits when their parents divorced. A variety of issues arise but can be dealt with satisfactorily (see Poor Kids[7]). The idea of FCI has popped up from time to time, only to be dismissed. This may be because Americans were convinced that ADC leads to divorce and separation, and believed the same of divorce insurance.[8] In the 1980s, proposals were introduced that had a family resemblance to FCI; they would have replaced ADC with an assured government payment for children linked to the strictest enforcement of parental support.[9]

widely used in teaching policy and more than a few people have told me that it influenced their choice of career.

The Negative Income Tax—A Wrong Solution

In 1965 and 1966, I was at the Office of Economic Opportunity (OEO) as a member of a small planning staff with a large charter: to plan for the government's anti-poverty activities and, in particular, for expenditures that would step slowly upwards to $14 billion a year. This scale of commitment was never nearly to be realized, of course. OEO's director, Sargent Shriver, came back from Lyndon Johnson's ranch in the spring of 1965 with word that the United States would be escalating the war in Vietnam; our planning goal would be scaled down very considerably.[11] Even so, we were a dedicated crew and in earnest about wiping out poverty.

One of the central ideas we considered was "welfare reform"; at the time, this meant substituting a negative income tax (NEGIT) for welfare. Offered as a preferable alternative to children's allowances, it accepts means testing as its core principle; so I opposed it.

In theory, NEGIT works like the income tax. A family reports its income; if it is less than a specified "guarantee," the family is paid half, say, of the deficit. The remaining half of the deficit, proponents argue, can only be reduced by earning more; thus, the formula is an incentive to work. NEGIT is visualized as a clerical if not a computer-managed operation and, so, is efficient and dignified.

There are technical problems, to be sure. In a debate about NEGIT that I had with James Tobin in *The Public Interest* in 1966, he conceded that there is "an inexorable dilemma" in designing such a program[12]: It is impossible to provide decent payments to people who have little or no income without paying at least a little to people who are far from poor. This means that a program with a decent payment level would be prohibitively expensive. Proponents struggle with this; in the end, they tend to dispose of the dilemma by muttering incantations such as "incremental" and "a foot in the door." However, the design "inexorably" prescribes that such a program could never go on to provide a decent level of income to the poor.

Walter Williams, one of the OEO planning staff members, commented as follows about the extended discussion that took place in our office. We were, he wrote:

> . . . engaged in an acrimonious debate over how welfare should be reformed. The choice was between a negative tax and a family allowance system. . . . Lined up in a solid front were the economists on the staff, including [himself], who argued that the negative income tax with its income test was the most effective means of getting money to the poor and that any realistic level of family allowance would provide only small dollar payments to the needy. . . . Against us was Alvin Schorr, a social worker by training. . . . He argued for the family allowance because it made payments a matter of right. . . . Schorr maintained at the time that whatever was done to build safeguards into a negative tax system . . ., it was likely to degenerate into a punitive welfare system. . . . The economists at OEO won the agency argument in that OEO in 1966 recommended a negative income tax to the president (which he did not accept) and thereafter fought within the inner circles of government for a negative tax as opposed to a family allowance. If we look at the years that have passed since our internal debate at OEO, there has been no strong evidence to refute the Schorr thesis. In fact, simply by laying the [1969 Nixon legislation for a negative income tax] on the table, I fear Mr. Schorr would win the debate hands down. . . .[13]

It was a handsome acknowledgment.[14]

As Williams noted, President Johnson did not accept the recommendation. Declining to accept defeat, OEO regularly submitted new versions of a negative income tax which the president as regularly ignored. At one point, a children's negative income tax was considered, which drew upon the relevant chapter in *Poor Kids*.[15]

Plans were laid for a campaign that looked beyond the current presidential term. Considering that most of the staff were carpetbagger academicians, inexperienced in government and politics, the steps that were taken showed imagination and strategic grasp. (I do not say this to take credit; that strategic thinking went on above my pay grade, as the saying goes.)

First, an income maintenance experiment was undertaken —the nation's first social science experiment, some claim—to test the effect of a negative income tax on work behavior. The study was scrupulously designed—maybe too scrupulously. The unexpected and, at first sight at least, unwelcome finding was that two kinds of people might somewhat *reduce* work activity if they were assured even a small income. These were women who would stay at home with young children and men who would decline low-paid work while seeking better wages. Upon reflection, however, one could not complain about this. Gathering such information was the ostensible reason for the studies, but I thought the more important reason was to legitimize the idea of the negative income tax and keep it alive in public consciousness.

Secondly, we undertook to establish an Institute for Research on Poverty—eventually settled at the University of Wisconsin. I do not take anything from the important work that has been done there over the years in offering my view that the impulse to establish the institute arose, in some large measure, from a desire to establish a center that would press forward work on a negative income tax.[16] Indeed, for some years, well into the era when it was clearly hopeless, the institute produced work supporting the establishment of a negative income tax.

Third, OEO proposed to President Johnson that he establish a President's Commission on Income Maintenance Programs. The commission was established with Ben W. Heineman, a Chicago industrialist, as chairman, Robert Harris as staff director and Nelson McClung as his deputy. Working, respectively, at HEW and the Treasury Department, Harris and McClung had been steadfast advocates of a negative income tax. We will continue this account further along.

I should not leave the impression that the OEO planning staff was occupied only with NEGIT. For example, we cosponsored a conference of housing experts with the Department of Housing and Urban Development with the purpose of finding ways to increase the housing available to poor people. As OEO was plainly not going to develop housing, we hoped to stimulate HUD to do more. At the conference we presented a proposal for subsidized home ownership for poor people. HUD economists treated this and other consequential proposals with polite disdain. Nor did they offer proposals. I thought the operating dynamic was resentment that tyros should presume to invade their turf. At one point, Charles Abrams, a widely known housing reformer and elder statesman in the field, rose to his feet, wagged an admonitory finger, and angrily observed that he had now discovered that HUD was "the enemy."

Also and to wider effect, the planning staff was deeply involved in manpower issues, in education, in community action, and in health and social services. Curiously, there seemed to be little interest in social security, which was providing over half the total income of poor people and, alone, kept three and a half million families out of poverty.

Social Security

Social security is a set of mainstream programs that had been enacted long since but, for the purposes of poor people, could

be strengthened. For example, before Congress enacted automatic cost of living adjustments in 1972, Congress enacted a
social security increase every two years—in time for each congressional election. Much depended on whether this was a
percentage increase (which would add less for the poor, who
were already receiving less), a flat sum for every beneficiary
(which would give the poor a larger share of the total cost of
the increase), or an increase in minimum benefit (90 percent of
which would go to poor people).

Because my colleagues were preoccupied with other matters, I found myself the sole representative of OEO in top-level
interagency meetings drafting recommendations for 1966 social
security legislation. I pressed for flat increases and, more than
that, for disproportionate increases in the minimum benefit.
One initial administration proposal called for a 15 percent
across-the-board increase in benefit levels and a minimum
benefit increase from $44 to $70. There finally emerged from
Congress a 13 percent increase in benefit levels and a $55
minimum benefit, the latter a 25 percent increase! About $4
billion was devoted to increases in 1967; how it was divided had
been worth some effort. (In the late 1970s, a wholly different
era, of course, social security amendments would virtually
eliminate minimum benefits.)

When I returned to HEW in 1967, as deputy assistant
secretary, I found a variety of ways to carry on the struggle for
children's allowances. We established a departmental task force
on "Exits from Poverty" which recommended a children's allowance. We helped the Citizens Committee for Children of
New York City stage an international conference on children's
allowances outside Washington.[17]

I had talked to Wilbur Cohen about children's allowances
in the early 1960s, while he was at the University of Michigan.
Now, as HEW undersecretary and then as secretary, he was
being urged by Alice Rivlin and others in his office to declare
for a negative income tax. I found occasions to make the case

for children's allowances. Once, I accompanied him to a closed hearing of the Heineman Commission. In the limousine en route, abandoning arguments of philosophy and principle, I pointed out that he had already established himself as the chief architect of security for the elderly in the United States. Now, he had an opportunity to do as much for children. He proved to be immune to such soft seduction.

At the hearing, Cohen confined himself to testifying about social security and declined to enter the welfare reform controversy. Heineman tried to draw him out on the subject of poverty among employable people, an implicit invitation to comment on—if not in favor of—the negative income tax and Cohen replied, "I don't have any such recommendation."

Exit from Government

Just before Richard Nixon's election as president, I was given a two-year leave of absence to take up a Ford Foundation grant to teach at Brandeis University and to provide consultation to "model cities" on the income maintenance component of their plans. ("Model cities" was a short-lived Johnson administration initiative to revive center cities; a comprehensive social plan was required for funding.) From time to time later on, when Washington seemed to be the very Sicily of corruption in government, I recalled with bemusement how painstakingly HEW's general counsel had considered whether it would violate conflict of interest regulations if I provided *free* consultation to model cities on matters that had been within my official responsibility.

In any event, the new secretary of HEW, Robert H. Finch, dismissed me on January 31, 1969, by a letter dated January 30, which I received after the fact. Though I thought dismissal natural and proper for a person in a policy role, this seemed an ungentlemanly display of haste. Anyway, I was now free of the constraints on expressing my opinion that I had felt.

We organized a group—Lisle Carter (who had earlier left

his position as assistant secretary), Eveline Burns, a well-known welfare economist, and others—which staged meetings in Atlanta, Minneapolis and New York to promote children's allowances. These meetings drew a respectable response that certainly owed something to their local sponsorship: the Atlanta Council of Social Agencies, Minnesota's former governor, Elmer L. Andersen, and the Citizens Committee for Children of New York.

FAP's Birth and Demise   In August 1969, to "a reluctant Congress," President Richard Nixon proposed "a sweeping income guarantee for families with children and a modest little welfare reform for the aged, blind, and disabled."[18] It was called the Family Assistance Plan (FAP). This proposal for a negative income tax closed months of internal argument, including heated opposition from people like Arthur F. Burns, economic counselor to the president.

Apparently influential in Nixon's affirmative decision was a staff memorandum from Daniel Patrick Moynihan, which argued that most of the money that might be in another year's budget had already been committed (much of it because we were at war in Vietnam, of course) and very little was available for a domestic initiative. If the president did not stake out his ground, available funds would "go down the drain" and Nixon would face reelection without being able to take credit for a single domestic initiative.[19]

The President's Commission on Income Maintenance, with staff leadership by Robert Harris and Nelson McClung, worked well into President Richard Nixon's term in office, issuing a report shortly after the president had proposed his own Family Assistance Program. It became obvious that they and White House staff headed by Moynihan had worked closely together so that the commission's recommendations, in effect, supported the president's.

I had for a little while been working with professor David Gil at Brandeis University to design and seek funding for a social experiment with a children's allowance. The administration had come into office encouraging experimentation with various forms of income maintenance. It seemed reasonable that, in the spirit of open scientific inquiry, a children's allowance should have a trial along with a negative income tax. Officials with the demonstration grant program at the Office of Economic Opportunity encouraged the idea,[20] but HEW, now committed to FAP, hotly opposed it.[21]

A month after the introduction of FAP, on September 12, the president directed that "henceforth no income maintenance experiment or demonstration be funded by any department or agency of the Federal government without the approval of [the White House]." The president explained that his concern was "that the results we look for not be diluted or distorted by a cacophony of competing 'findings' and claims from the parallel and competitive experiments now beginning to spring up on every hand."[22] The letter exhibited a certain irritation and I thought that its phrasing owed something to Moynihan. At any rate, it disposed of the children's allowance experiment—and social science, as well.

The country now had a concrete plan—indeed, two plans: the president's and the Heineman Commission's. I spoke and wrote widely in opposition to them, pointing out problems that were no longer speculative. For example, much had been made of NEGIT's efficiency; it was said that it could direct money to poor people without wasting it on others. The Heineman Commission proposed a program that would pay $3,600 a year to a family of four with no other income. (The poverty level for a family of four was about $3,900 a year.) With a design that reduced payments by $1 for each $2 of earnings, families with income up to $7,200 would have received payments. Calculation showed that 36 percent of program expenditures would have gone to poor families; that is, the program would have been 36 percent efficient.[23]

This was markedly less efficient than existing social secu-

rity, which NEGIT proponents had been impugning as inefficient. The president's FAP arrived at virtually 100 percent efficiency by providing a scant $1,600 for a family of four. Thus was
illustrated Tobin's "inexorable dilemma": NEGIT is efficient
only at derisory levels of assistance.

Looking back on this period several years later, Alice
Rivlin drew this moral:

> Solving the income maintenance problem will re-
> quire more than coming up with neat sounding
> proposals. It will be necessary to think these propos-
> als through carefully, to explore how they would
> relate to existing programs and how they would be
> administered.
>
> . . . I am not saying that the policy analysts of 1966
> were politically naive—worse than that, we were
> technically naive. We were like theoretical physicists
> trying to build a bridge or a bomb. We simply did not
> understand how complicated practical problems
> were. Now that we do, perhaps progress will be
> faster.[24]

With an explicit plan on display, practical problems like the
proposed "guarantee" level surfaced one after another.

Mitchell Ginsberg, New York City's human resources administrator and a widely acknowledged social work leader,
took a prominent part in trying to negotiate an acceptable FAP.
He had been introduced at the White House as Mayor John F.
Lindsay's representative, after Senators Abraham Ribicoff and
Edward Kennedy asked Mayor Lindsay to make him available.
Ginsberg invented a role for himself as the representative of a
variety of interest groups: welfare administrators, social workers, client advocates and organized labor. These groups were
not without differences, of course. For some months, he con-

ducted what I came to refer to as Mitchell Ginsberg's Floating FAP Game.

Ginsberg would bring together representatives of various constituencies at some hospitable site in Washington and invite reactions to FAP and to congressional and administration ideas for perfecting it. He would find consensus at these meetings, although inquiry would have revealed that the consensus had uncertain formal status. (But no one asked.) Ginsberg would then use this "consensus" to negotiate with congressional leaders and the administration. I was dubious about this enterprise, thinking that it implied support for some form of FAP and that FAP would turn out badly. Still, I participated in his Floating FAP Game—out of pleasure in watching Ginsberg operate and from fear that FAP might get enacted. If so, surely I ought to participate in trying to improve it.

The National Welfare Rights Organization (NWRO) played a prominent role opposing FAP; its opposition took the form of demanding changes that Congress would not conceivably entertain: a $6,500 minimum guarantee and abandoning work requirements, for example. In coalition with civil rights leaders, NWRO seemed more influential than its numbers or resources might otherwise have commanded. I was concerned that NWRO was expending its energies on trying to improve FAP without having realizable, long-term objectives.

In 1969 I invited the executive director of NWRO, George Wiley, to spend an afternoon in conversation. I spelled out what might be achieved for his constituency by an alternative strategy: barely noticeable technical adjustment of social security benefits, enactment of a children's allowance and other mainstream measures. He appeared to be somewhat persuaded, but finally said candidly that welfare and FAP were excellent organizing targets. They mobilized ready-made constituencies. Unfortunately, what I was talking about was complex and did not readily lend itself to organizing methods. For him, this had to be determining.

(Nevertheless, some years later George Wiley left NWRO to organize the Movement for Economic Justice, with objectives similar to those I had been urging on him. Sadly, in 1973 he drowned while boating in Chesapeake Bay.)

For a congressman (later longtime mayor of Minneapolis) who was especially interested in children, Donald Fraser, I outlined legislation which would provide a "pre-school children's allowance." Seeking to promote "take-off" for young families while limiting program expenditures, it provided an allowance for pre-school children and then moved the allowance up one year at a time to seven, eight, and so forth. Thus, in the end, all children would be covered. Fraser introduced the bill "for discussion," as he said.

I helped draft a speech endorsing children's allowances that Senator George McGovern was to deliver at a meeting of the Citizens Committee for Children in New York City in January 1970. Obviously, he was trying out what might become a campaign theme. But there was a hitch. It turned out that Jesse Jackson, who was advising the senator, was cool to the idea of children's allowances. With McGovern's consent, I flew out to Chicago to talk to Jackson. Laid up in bed with a broken leg, he listened and examined the issue for two hours. I left without knowing what he had concluded. Upon my return to Washington, I was given word to proceed with drafting the speech. In New York, McGovern's speech got a warm reception that encouraged him to pursue the matter—briefly. Subsequent audiences quickly made apparent their concern with the birth-rate issue, an objection that would be fatal to the chances of a children's allowance—and to the political ambitions of anyone who promoted it.

In testimony for the U.S. Senate Select Committee on Nutrition and Human Needs in 1970, I took occasion to point out a hidden objective that lay behind arguments for a negative income tax: the division of social security into two programs. One would be similar to private insurance, paying benefits proportional to

the taxes one had paid, which is to say proportional to one's
former income. If, from time to time, the government added an
adjustment for inflation, as it does, middle-income and wealthy
people would have a very good thing, indeed.

The second part of social security would be carefully
limited to poor people. It would provide benefits as decent
as possible within the limits of congressional anxiety about
whether recipients would continue to work, whether they
might have children out of wedlock, and so forth. This would
effectively remove millions of people from the statutory protection of social security and entrust them to the tender mercies of
a new welfare program, renamed FAP or NEGIT or whatever—
conceivably even a program devolved to states.*

This view about splitting social security was explicit in the
report of the Heineman Commission, in the work of a congressional committee chaired by Martha Griffiths, a Democrat of
Michigan, and in the work of economists such as Joseph Pechman and Alicia Munnell.[25] The net effect would have been a
transfer of public funds from the poor to the middle class.

Fortunately, mainstream social security was so broadly
popular and its constituency so powerful politically that such
radical change was simply not feasible, with or without a
negative income tax and however it might have benefited
elements of the constituency. To be sure, since the 1970s social
security has been somewhat skewed to the interests of those
who are better off. Enactment of automatic *percentage* cost-of-
living increases and elimination of the minimum benefit are
examples. However, the economists' dream of two separate
programs, each more purely devoted to its special objective,
faded peacefully away—for some years, at least.

In the end, in the fall of 1972, FAP went down to defeat in
Congress. In dwelling on my own activities, I may have given

---

*In 1996, we finally came to devolution of welfare in the United States, but at least
the poor elderly, disabled, widowed and orphaned have not been stripped of social
security benefits.*

the impression that the country was largely opposed to it. Actually, there was much support: from liberals and so-called liberal newspapers, who saw in FAP a "foot in the door," that is, a commitment to a "guaranteed income" that might eventually be improved to a reasonable level; from conservatives who saw an opportunity to wipe out "the welfare system" or felt that they ought to support the president; and from many who simply felt that welfare had to be replaced.

Defeat was followed by much passing around of blame, as if someone unpleasant had died but now everyone felt guilty. I thought that intense national debate and the attempt to develop a bill had exposed ambiguities and difficulties that made it clear that the idea was unworkable. The last versions of the bill ran to hundreds of pages and, as an AFL-CIO lobbyist, Bertrand Russell Seidman, testified to the House Ways and Means Committee, no one, not he nor any member of Congress, could understand the bill.

I thought, besides, that the president had never been enthusiastic about the idea and had deserted it in the end.[26] This view was confirmed when his chief of staff, H. R. (Bob) Haldeman, published his diary. His notes for the diary quoted the president telling him to kill FAP and blame its death on the Democrats.[27]

As I look back, it intrigues me—more than intriguing me, it blows my mind—to consider that ideas like the negative income tax and splitting social security, incubating mainly in academia, prefigured the drive to radical income inequality that was to come to fruition in the 1980s. I do not accuse these academics of plotting such redistribution; indeed, economists such as James Tobin and Joseph Pechman identified themselves as egalitarians. I merely observe that their ideas were assimilated into and fostered developments that would promote inequality. Ronald Reagan did not entirely *lead* the country to radical inequality; he rode a tide in the affairs of men that led on to fortune for the fortunate. But what swelled the tide in the first place?

Some theories have it that these matters go in cycles—thirty-year cycles, for example.[28] Yet, what is the mechanism that produces each new cycle? The current cycle, beginning to emerge in the 1960s, must represent the experience and views of generations born in the 1930s and immediately after. Growing up during or just after the Depression, living through World War II, starting a family and beginning employment just after the war[29]—how would these experiences produce a generation and, especially, a generation of their children whose values were perfectly exemplified by Ronald Reagan and—not to overlook that the trend to inequality was international—Margaret Thatcher?, I ask, truly puzzled.

"On the Knocking on the Gate . . ."

In Shakespeare's *Macbeth*, after the king has been murdered, Lady Macbeth tries to steady her agitated husband. Transfixed with the horror of his deed, Macbeth ruminates that "all great Neptune's ocean" will not wash the blood from his hand. Abruptly, a pounding on the gate alarms everyone, yet does not seem to advance the play. Scholars fret about Shakespeare's reason for introducing it. In a famous essay, Thomas De Quincey argued that the ordinary, surrounding world must be brought onto the stage so one may feel how shocking the staged drama is.[30]

In the matters I have been describing, it was just the other way around. Around our relatively peaceful work and small-scale intellectual and political skirmishing, the country was at war in Vietnam and with itself. Drama and tragedy were everywhere. Fires and riots burned in the ghettoes of our cities. Student protesters ringed the White House and took control of campuses, seeking an end to the war. Martin Luther King and Robert Kennedy were assassinated. The Chicago Seven clashed with police during the Democratic National Convention in Chicago, disorder for which the police were as responsible as the students.

These matters touched our work in ways small and large. When I was asked to scout out a venue for President Johnson's speech on welfare, I realized that almost anywhere he gave a commencement speech in the spring of 1968, we could expect unruly demonstrations. One day, the HEW building was closed because of a bomb threat. I have referred to the radio call-in show I listened to as I drove home; and I wondered whether our society was worth saving. At a meeting in the White House, Wilbur Cohen kept standing up and looking out the window. When I asked what he was looking for, he explained that demonstrators had circled the White House; he was trying to see if he could pick out his son among them.

More important than incidents, of course, was the reality that the conduct of the war in Vietnam made it impossible to spend what was needed at home. Even though Lyndon Johnson was determined to spend for guns *and* butter, there simply was not enough money.

The 1960s afforded a historic opportunity for reform and democratization. The country's affluence, the spirit of Camelot, the civil rights movement, the nationwide outrage and guilt at the assassination of John F. Kennedy, and the rare capacities and convictions of Lyndon Johnson which flowered when he was president, all coming together, might have made us a finer country. The war in Vietnam undermined this, of course. The oncoming stagflation undermined this. The greedy and vindictive tide that ran just under the surface undermined this. The damage that we did instead of reform will mark us for decades.

Segue

I was weary of Washington. It came to seem to me that Washington is a courtesan. If you are a member of the court, she will cosset and oblige you in ways you have not dreamt of. When there is a new king, she moves on without a backward glance. She has her vocation and she performs it well. I had had extraordinary years in Washington and I was grateful for them.

What I had learned is not taught in any school I know. Most important, I now recognized that I was opposing a tide, not simply an accidental accumulation of shortsighted or misguided individuals.

In 1970, I walked across the Ellipse behind the White House and talked to the young people lying there peacefully, passing around "joints"—an affront to busy officials and tourists alike. I know it is not fashionable to like and respect those students—many are themselves embarrassed about their acts in the 1960s—but I thought they were the hope of the future. I decided that I would moderate my attentions to the generations in power and address myself to the next generations. I was offered the position of dean of the Graduate School of Social Work at New York University and I thought, yes, I will do that.

NOTES

1. Alvin L. Schorr, *Social Security and Social Services in France,* Government Printing Office, Washington, D.C., 1965.

2. Christiane Rochefort, *Les Petits Enfants due Siècle,* Bernard Grasset, Paris, 1961.

3. "Social Scientists' Advisory Meeting, Summary of Deliberations, June 20–21, 1960," Social Security Administration, Washington, D.C. Mimeographed. Published as "Priorities in Family Life," *Papers in Social Welfare,* no. 3, Brandeis University, Waltham, Massachusetts.

4. Participants in the meeting held in 1965 by the Social Security Administration were Vincent Whitney, chairman, Irene Taeuber, Ronald Freedman, Arthur Campbell and Nathan Keyfitz.

5. Alvin L. Schorr, "Income and the Birth Rate," *Social Security Bulletin,* December 1965. With small changes, the same essay appears as Chapter 5 in *Poor Kids,* Basic Books, New York, 1966, pp. 77-78, 84.

6. Vincent H. Whitney, "Fertility Trends and Children's Allowance Programs," in Eveline M. Burns, ed., *Children's Allowances and the Economic Welfare of Children,* Citizens Committee for Children, New York, 1968.

7. Alvin L. Schorr, *Poor Kids,* Basic Books, New York, 1966. The paraphrased statement appears in W. W. Rostow, *The Stages of Economic Growth,* Cambridge University Press, Cambridge, U.K., 1960, p. 470.

8. For a comment on fatherless child insurance, see President's Commission on Income Maintenance Programs, *Background Papers,* Chapter 4, "Restructuring Social Insurance," Government Printing Office, Washington, D.C., 1969, pp. 442–45. See also Alvin L. Schorr, "The Socially Orphaned . . . Next Step in Social Security," *New York Times,* Sunday Magazine Section, 1 November 1965.

9. Irwin Garfinkel, Sara McLanahan, and Philip Robins, eds., *Child Support Assurance: Design Issues, Expected Impacts, and Political Barriers as Seen from Wisconsin,* Urban Institute Press, Washington, D.C., 1992.

10. *The Economist* (London), v. 222, 7 January 1967, p. 44.

11. For a summary of the income maintenance debate by the planning staff's director, see Joseph A. Kershaw (with the assistance of Paul N. Courant), *Government Against Poverty,* The Brookings Institution, Washington, D.C., 1970, Chapter 6; also, pp. 165–66.

12. James Tobin, "The Case for an Income Guarantee," *The Public Interest,* no. 4, Summer 1966, pp. 31–44. My rejoinder, "Against a Negative Income Tax," appeared in v. 2, Fall 1966.

13. Walter Williams, "The Case for the Negative Income Tax: The Second Time Around," Institute of Governmental Research, Public Policy Paper no. 3, University of Washington, Seattle, March 1972, p. 14.

14. Kershaw, op. cit.

15. Kershaw, op. cit.

16. Robert A. Levine, who became director of the planning office after Joseph Kershaw left, writes regarding this comment about "the impulse to establish the Institute": "I think that's wrong. The timing was such that the Institute was begun (work started in early 1965) before the NEGIT was taken seriously. When the [income maintenance] experiment was conceived, [Sargent Shriver] insisted we put it there. We did not disagree."

17. Eveline M. Burns, ed., *Children's Allowances and the Economic Welfare of Children,* Citizens' Committee for Children of New York, New York, 1968.

18. Vincent J. and Vee Burke, *Nixon's Good Deed—Welfare Reform,* Columbia University Press, New York, 1974.

19. Daniel Patrick Moynihan, Memorandum for the President, "Comment on Paul W. McCracken's Memorandum, 'A Possible Resolution of the Welfare Reform Controversy,' " 6 June 1969. Cited in Vincent J. and Vee Burke, *Nixon's Good Deed—Welfare Reform,* Columbia University Press, New York, 1974, p. 82.

20. David G. Gil, *Unravelling Social Policy,* Schenkman Books, Rochester,

Vermont, revised 4th ed., 1990, pp. 137–38. On p. 148 is a quotation from OEO's 1969 budget document noting plans to fund a children's allowance demonstration.

21. Richard L. Strout, "Nixon Aides Argue Merits of Family-Aid Plans," *Christian Science Monitor,* Weekend issue, 21–23 June 1969.

22. Quoted in Alvin L. Schorr, Memorandum to Model City Directors, "The Family Assistance Program, Its Meaning to Model Cities," 20 October 1969.

23. *Poverty Amid Plenty: The American Paradox,* The President's Commission on Income Maintenance Programs, Government Printing Office, Washington, D.C., 1969, Table 5, p. 62.

24. Alice M. Rivlin, Discussion of papers by James Tobin and Robert J. Lampman, paper presented at the Annual Meeting of the American Statistical Association, New York, 27–30 December 1973; *Proceedings,* American Statistical Association, Washington, D.C., 1974.

25. Using technical language, to be sure, Alicia Munnell wrote, ". . . that the earnings replacement and welfare functions [of social security] could be fulfilled more efficiently if they were performed by two separate programs." "The Carter Proposals for Social Security," *Challenge,* 20, no. 4, September–October 1977, pp. 57–58.

26. Alvin L. Schorr, "Who Killed Cock Robin Hood?", *Harper's Magazine,* June 1973.

27. Fred Emery, author of *Watergate: The Corruption of American Politics and the Fall of Richard Nixon,* speaking at a luncheon meeting of the City Club of Cleveland, 26 August 1994. Emery found this observation in Haldeman's notes for his diary, though it was not carried in the published work.

28. Arthur M. Schlesinger, Jr., *The Cycles of History,* Houghton Mifflin, Boston, 1986. See also Kevin P. Phillips, *The Politics of the Rich and the Poor: Wealth and the American Electorate in the Reagan Aftermath,* Random House, New York, 1990.

29. For a longitudinal study of how living through the Depression affected the lives and attitudes of families, see Glen H. Elder, *Children of the Great Depression: Social Change in Life Experience,* University of Chicago Press, Chicago, 1974.

30. Thomas De Quincey, "On the Knocking on the Gate in Macbeth," *Macbeth, A Casebook,* John Wain, ed., Macmillan and Co., London, 1968, pp. 90–93.

You Win Some!
You Lose Some!
NYU and McGovern

On a sunny Labor Day in 1970, I arrived at the house in Greenwich Village that New York University was providing for us. We had to make our way through throngs of people who had come for Washington Square's annual art fair, but I imagined that they were putting on a welcoming party. The house, badly abused by students who stayed there while its tenant traveled abroad, required top-to-bottom renovation. So we had the pleasure of a virtually new home just north of the square. My wife, often prescient, had said when I talked to her about moving, "Can we take the house and not the job?"

There were many problems attached to the NYU Graduate School of Social Work at the time. The body that accredits schools of social work, the Council on Social Work Education, had postponed reaccreditation for three years, pointing to poorly integrated classroom courses and fragmented, poorly supervised field work instruction. The students had staged school-wide strikes for three consecutive years, mainly protesting racism in school administration, and were shortly to stage another. And the government was preparing to cut back on financial support. We were going to find out if less is really better. Faculty morale was poor.

Although I had taught from time to time, I had never been a full-time faculty member; for practical purposes, I was new to academia. At first, I was baffled by uncertain lines of authority and responsibility. In theory, we were collegial, that is, the faculty was a town-meeting-style democracy. This meant that virtually any decision could be debated and postponed. Since many of the choices facing us at the time were unpleasant, the task of choosing among them tended to drift on indefinitely. If, finally, the dean imposed a choice, there would be much talk of highhandedness and flouting faculty prerogatives.

After I had been at NYU a little while, I observed to the president, James M. Hester, that no one seemed to be in charge; he took umbrage. He said that *he* was in charge. But the truth, as nearly as I could make it out, was that he carefully consulted faculties and deans on every serious matter, trying to form a consensus; and he rarely acted if he could not gather one. Providing leadership in a university requires talent and vast stores of patience; Hester seemed to have both—and class besides. I quite liked him and this helped when, later, unavoidably, I found myself pitted against him.

Year 1   With the considerable help of an experienced and devoted associate dean, Shirley Ehrenkranz, we moved on several fronts that first year. A problem in teaching social work students is that, in the end, they take disparate jobs—from dealing as caseworkers with abandoned children or demented elderly people to administering or advising on broad government policies. Therefore, it is difficult to devise a common introductory curriculum, as the Council on Social Work Education had recommended. Especially is it difficult because each professor has a vested interest in continuing to teach just as she has taught. Nevertheless, we worked out a so-called generic curriculum, and brought it off with more general agreement and sense of excitement than might have been expected.

Typically, social work students spend two or three days a week in settings where, under close supervision, they begin to do the work they will do. The council had criticized our arrangements for this field work, and so we planned training centers—at the NYU Medical Center and at New York City's Human Resources Administration, to begin with—where groups of students could receive a better integrated and supervised work experience. We also moved towards order in the school's internal arrangements—codifying procedures about how the school was governed, about student files, about personnel.

All these tasks I had more or less expected, but chronic student strikes turned out to be symptomatic of a deep-seated problem for which I was not prepared. For example, a professor I shall call William Armstrong stopped by my office to urge me to take a firm position on how student grades should be awarded. As in many schools at the time, A's and B's were handed out freely and grades had come to be meaningless. Faculty should be more rigorous, Armstrong opined. I quite agreed and asked him to speak up when the matter would be discussed at faculty meeting. "Don't count on me, Alvin," he said, and went on to explain.

In a Midwestern university where Armstrong once taught, he had supported a faculty member unjustly accused of radical activity. Thereafter, Armstrong was subject to suspicion himself and, in time, forced to resign. Though faculty members had privately encouraged his stand, none now came to his defense. Then he took a job in Washington. "Do you remember," Armstrong asked rhetorically, "when the Klan burned a cross on someone's lawn in [suburban] Kensington and the community got together to fight the Klan? Not me! I sold my house and moved." He would not now risk drawing the students' anger.

Armstrong may have been more traumatized than other faculty, but in fact the faculty generally were fearful of the students and inclined to give way to them rather than to stand for standards or principles. This is a grave observation, so one must bear the time and context in mind: not long after the reign of Senator Joseph McCarthy and on the heels of widespread student militance which, at NYU, had included a seriously regarded threat to blow up computer facilities.

These pressures came together at our school around a faculty procedure for reviewing the performance of students.

Not all students who are admitted to social work school are suitable for graduation as professional social workers. Student performance was reviewed by a faculty committee and some students were "intermitted," that is, invited to drop out for a semester or a year. In practice, few asked to return. Student activists, joined at times by a Black Faculty Caucus, focused on securing procedural changes—including, most significantly, several student representatives on the review committee. Student strikes supported demands for such changes, and year by year the faculty yielded one point and then another. In the early 1960s, about fifteen students were intermitted each year; by 1971, only one or two.

I was greatly concerned about what was at play in annual student strikes and in faculty-student relations. The students operated from various motives, including an earnest desire to make society's institutions more responsive to constituents. (We had such students because we wanted them.) They thought that sincerity and belligerency alone would carry the day; they seemed to be learning that it was so.

The students overlooked the fact that, while in the end their teachers would protect them, future employers or adversaries might not. Moreover, they were not yet equipped with the fact-finding and organizing skills for activism that we hoped to teach them in class. It was alarming to me that students might be perceiving that, in dealing with them, in some measure faculty members were forsaking their own standards. The education by example that students were receiving was probably more powerful than anything that went on in class. In real life or in real work, chances were, many would quickly get hurt and not a few would turn cynical.

I urged the faculty to remember that they were in charge, if they wanted to be, and that they owed to their profession a truly deliberative process for "counseling out" students who should not continue. There was some disposition to rise to the challenge, and some fear. In the end, the faculty voted to do away with the review process and work out a new process during the summer. It was well understood that this might provoke another student strike in the next year.

Year 2   The second year held difficulties and promise. In response to financial cuts, five faculty members had to be given notice. During their terminal year these five would constitute an aggrieved cabal; then there would be an extra load for faculty who continued. Minority enrollment, which stood at about one-third, declined slightly because of declining scholarship funds. The students talked about a strike over the issue of the new review procedure but the faculty held their ground and, for the first time in five years, there was no strike. A new second-year curriculum was completed, to follow on the new first-year curriculum, and planning was also undertaken for a new under-graduate social work program. The capacity of the faculty to complete this work contributed to a growing sense of cohesion.

All this progress was quite overwhelmed by develop-ments in the university, which now faced a financial crisis that had been coming on for some time. The president named a task force of deans to recommend remedial action—including one from every school with a deficit except Social Work. Reading the tea leaves, I immediately wrote to him that this was a "hanging" task force. I asked that our school be represented—by myself, by our former dean, or by an outside social work educator. He added another dean—from the Law School. A bad sign!

Midway through the 1971–72 school year, the task force recommended closing the Schools of Engineering and Social Work. Social Work's deficit was $200,000 a year, a derisory sum even then and a trivial portion of the university's overall deficit. Closing the Social Work School must have been hard for Hester to accept. His presidency had been based on promoting NYU as an "urban university," with social work central to its mission. Nevertheless, he supported closing.

The announcement that a school is to be closed is like a voodoo curse: No weapon is needed; a school thrashes about and dies. Forward planning was brought to a halt. There were resignations on virtually no notice and candidates withdrew their applications for positions. Obviously, there would be difficulty recruiting students for the next year. Such a crisis can push a faculty apart or bring it together. Fortunately, this one brought the faculty together.

Trying to piece together what was really happening, I talked to a member of the New York State Board of Regents, Kenneth B. Clark. Clark was unsurprised: For well over a year NYU's chancellor, Allan Cartter, had been consulting with the regents about closing the school. In other words, closing the school was under active consideration when I was offered the position of dean. I recalled bitterly the bait that Hester had dangled. Sensing my hesitation and guessing that I must be hoping that the next election would restore to office a Democratic administration to which I could return, he said, "Why don't you accept the deanship for three years, anyway?"

I assessed the school's problem like this: Our deficit was picayune. Moreover, analysis of the books, opened to us after much resistance, made it clear that even the small deficit attributed to us was inflated with wholly unreasonable costs—for example, a share of the deficits of other schools! Other schools were given three years to show a balanced budget; only Engineering and Social Work were excepted. Social Work's problem was not primarily, if at all, financial.

In the 1970s, NYU emerged from a period of highly successful fund-raising into a straitened government and philanthropic climate. Deficits mounted. University administration was now criticized for spendthrift policies and loose controls. Deans of schools without deficits, fearing that they would bear the burden for others, were particularly incensed. They focused their complaints on the president. Charges of loose administration reverberated in philanthropic circles; university fund-raisers were met with sharp questions and skepticism.

So university administrators needed to tighten up—that is, needed *to be seen* to tighten up; the two schools were selected for show and tell. Probably, Engineering was a target because applications for admission had been declining in response to a nationwide drop in demand for engineers; and because it occupied its own valuable and expensive-to-maintain campus in the Bronx, which the state was interested in buying. The sale price would cover NYU's deficit for several years. As for Social Work, it was a small, troubled school, lacking wealthy or influential alumni. *Who would miss it and its hippie students!* I speculated, also, that closing Social Work was a sacrifice demanded of the president—as of Abraham—to demonstrate his determination to hew to rigorous policies.

I reflected grandly that I had not come to the school to preside over its liquidation. We would fight. The campaign began with meetings with the president in which I tried futilely to persuade him that his decision was unreasonable. Then we moved to discussions of how the viability of the school might yet be demonstrated. Hester suggested that he might reconsider his decision if we could raise $1 million in an emergency campaign. (In later years, $1 million would sound like petty cash, but for a social work school at the time it was a heroic figure.) The president's proposal had considerable merit for us: If we could bring it off, the success should demonstrate our "new" fiscal correctness. More important, fund-raising would move the matter from an intramural dispute onto a public stage. There, perhaps, the political balance could be shifted.

The campaign to save the school began vigorously but civilly. It took a little time to rise to the level of a row. A member of the school's advisory committee called me a couple of days after I had discussed fund-raising with the committee. With more than a hint of doubt in his voice, he asked if I was serious. "These people don't know anything about fund-raising," he said, "and [pausing] neither do you." "So, help us," I said. Joseph Willen had been passive and bored in meetings, but it turned out that he was a retired fund-raiser with a considerable reputation. He called again a couple of days later. The chancellor had told him that he didn't know why I was so exercised: I had been assured that, in any case, there would be a position for me. This inflamed me and I said I had not come to NYU to feather my nest. Willen was impressed. Several days later, I received from him a several-page, single-spaced letter, detailing the steps we would have to take.

Willen persuaded a friend who was a well-connected lawyer, David Sher, to chair a fund-raising committee. University rules did not permit us to solicit gifts from NYU trustees, who were our best prospects, of course, so Willen and Sher set about securing an exception. Naturally, this effort required that trustees hear and think about the school. We worked out a list of prospects and began approaching them. I had taught research but Willen's research taught me new lessons. He knew everything about a prospect before a call was made—how much money he had, how much she gave and to whom, his frailties, her ambitions.

Willen met with the faculty to explain how we should go about fund-raising. I recall some of his homilies: *If an organization sends a resolution of support, forget them; they are not going to give. If you are offered an unsolicited check, give it back; it is not enough.* He was funny, skillful and tough.

We prepared press releases and I spoke everywhere I could get an invitation. Though not always of a single mind, New York's large social welfare community, intricately woven into the fabric of the city, united to help—offering contributions, letters, intercession with people who had some role in this matter. Not signaled beforehand, a check for $10,000 arrived from the Atran Foundation. This gift was particularly impressive because Atran was a substantial supporter of the Yeshiva University School of Social Work, which was suffering its own financial difficulties. (Willen's advice notwithstanding, we did not return the check.) Nor were we totally lacking in influential supporters who would intervene on our behalf—for example, Ruth Farkas, U.S. ambassador to Luxembourg, an NYU alumna and major contributor.

In the midst of our travails, I was summoned into the street to watch firemen try to douse a blaze in the school's administration building. Vivid in my mind was a vision of our applications for admission, rank on rank, in file cases in the midst of the fire. If they went up in smoke, many could not be reconstructed. The building had once been a residence for artists, some of whom stayed on at controlled rents after the university took over the building. An elderly woman emerged from the flaming building, clutching a robe, with gray hair flying. She leveled a trembling, arthritic finger at me and accused me of setting the fire to get rid of the tenants. All at once, briskly, it began to snow. It was like a Cecil B. De Mille movie and I knew my lines. I threw up my arms to the wide, dark sky and proclaimed that "I get the message."

Hester now reported that money was coming in; perhaps it would be enough to turn the decision around. For my part, I was alarmed at the internal damage the school was suffering and urged that he turn his sanguine prediction into a public announcement. As we approached summer, with no new decision and matters looking better on the outside but worse on the inside, I asked that the University Senate take up the issue.

Hester called me to object. *You want the senate to reverse my decision,* he said. Not at all, I said, I simply wanted them to give him their best advice. *If you go ahead with this, you will lose my confidence.* I said that it seemed to me that he wanted the school quietly to commit suicide. If these were our sole options, I preferred that the school be murdered. My wife and daughter stood in the corner of our living room, listening, and cheered when I hung up.

The senate meeting was not polite. I described the progress we had been making until the task force's blow fell. I reviewed "the small, shoddy study by an internationally known public finance expert" on which the task force's recommendation was based. Aroused, the task force chairman, dean Dick Netzer, defended the study. In the long, painful meeting only one senator, Oscar Ornati, a manpower economist, supported the school. Ornati made a brief statement, indicating that in the future there would be an extensive labor market need for social workers.

A student senator from the Business School observed that since the country did not care about social work, it was hard to see why, "at a time like this," the university should invest in something the country did not care about. Throughout the controversy, the administration had been saying that the school's problem was purely financial: The school's quality was not an issue. Now, the chancellor said it was not a good school, anyway. I wondered aloud at the desperation that led him to inject this gratuitous insult at the last moment. As he understood very well, it would be damaging to people who might shortly be looking for work.

We asked that the senate vote the school up or down: Either restore its franchise fully or take responsibility for seeing it closed. As may be the way of university senates everywhere, it temporized, recommending that the matter be reconsidered in the fall.

Denouement   During the summer, several hundred thousand dollars was raised in gifts and pledges—I never knew exactly how much—and it seemed we might reach our goal of $1 million. Yet, all our faculty had been given formal letters of termination. Technically, these could be rescinded but, naturally, faculty members were anxious. We lost faculty and could not hire replacements. Funding could not be arranged for the field work training centers we had been planning, and host institutions withdrew from sponsorship. It even appeared that our government funding might be interrupted. Though still united and determined, the faculty was showing strain. Once more, I asked for a declaration that the school would continue, but the president would not take this step.

In a climactic exchange for me, I said that he was urging us to gamble on success, asking that we carry on because things looked good. If Hester thought our chances so good, then the university should take a gamble. I asked that the school be given a clean start in the fall; if not, I would resign. With no change at the end of the summer, I did so. Twice, at Hester's request, I reconsidered and then resigned finally, effective the following January.

Now the university had to go one way or the other. Considerations that influenced the president must have included the changed political situation: the school's mission and danger now more prominent and support for it now more evident. Perhaps Hester's original commitment to the school also re-emerged. When the university began a search for a new dean, it was plain that the school would survive. No one would accept the position without assurances to that effect.

The school did survive and two decades later is thriving both academically and financially. (The Engineering School was closed, however.) After two more deans came and went, the faculty nominated associate dean Shirley Ehrenkranz as a candidate for the position. She was dean for many years and, in time, the school was named for her.

The SIMP Center   From my beginning at NYU, I believed that, for reasons good and bad, the need for social workers would expand greatly beyond the availability of people with Master of Social Work degrees. Undergraduate programs would have to expand considerably, as indeed they have. In order to provide the teachers and other leaders that such growth would require, doctoral programs would also have to expand.

But starting a Ph.D. program was not the school's most urgent priority. As a preliminary step, I proposed to establish a policy center that could form the core of a doctoral program when the time came. Conceived as a Center for Studies in Income Maintenance Policy (SIMP Center), it would do research and analysis on policies relevant to people's income:

work, taxation, social security. With Hester's help—this was before the news about closing the school descended—financing was assembled from the Milbank Memorial Fund, the Rockefeller Brothers Fund, and the Rockefeller Foundation.

The timing was not auspicious. We began assembling center faculty and setting up offices more or less as I was leaving the school. Although it was intended that center faculty should teach at the school, regular school faculty tended to regard the center as my purely personal project. The faculty were angry at me for deserting them, as many of them saw it, and so collegial relationships with center faculty never developed. The center was financed for three years, after which the school let it expire.

The center had appointed some very good people, both faculty (Winifred Bell and Martha Ozawa) and consultant economists (Robert Lekachman and Charlotte Muller). With some others, we turned out a series of pamphlets with chrome yellow covers on income distribution, welfare policy, employment policy, taxation, social security, social services and health care that made these matters accessible to students and informed lay people.[1] The pamphlets were widely circulated. I learned years later that the discussion paper series of the important "welfare state programme" at the London School of Economics had taken inspiration from ours. Martha Ozawa, in particular, developed a set of ideas about social security that she deepened and developed, winning growing recognition during subsequent years.[2]

By the time of its expiration, the center had assembled a book called *Jubilee for Our Times*.[3] It set forth an incremental program for reducing income inequality, relying on established mechanisms and only two or three new ideas; one of them is now enshrined in tax law as the earned income tax credit. The book proposed shifting $55 to $60 billion from higher-income to lower-income people in a manner that would have raised the income share of the poorest fifth of the population from 5 percent to 10 percent.

It would be meaningless to talk now about the difference that these particular changes might have made, but a nation that so much as *wished* to implement such changes twenty years ago might not so painfully be deploring the disappearance of community today.

How It Seemed   I had come to New York to address myself to younger generations and had done precious little of this. I heard from our students chiefly through non-negotiable demands and graffiti ("Schorr is a racist dean") and saw them primarily during demonstrations and confrontations. Though we had started out hopefully together, in the end the faculty were angry at me. Day by day, I found less to enjoy in this position than in any of several difficult positions I had held. I did and do take very great satisfaction in the survival and eventual success of the school.

The feeling that I brought from Washington that the country was moving into a hard time was reinforced. In microcosm, the move to close the school reflected a swelling national impatience with the poor and their pathos. What the student senator had said was true or was about to be true: The country did not care about poor people.

In all times, those who deal with poor and disadvantaged people—social workers, public housing administrators, legal aid lawyers—share in their relative powerlessness and stigma. Indeed, it is one of the problems of poor people that those closest to them, who could otherwise help them, are distrusted and looked down upon by professional colleagues and the public. So I thought that social work schools everywhere were going to have to struggle for survival. Yet, it had also become plain that simultaneously the content and quality of instruction would have to be improved.

Many of our troubles at NYU were common in other schools of social work, though I thought our student protest lasted longer than elsewhere and was more ingenuous. I emerged with the conviction that it is reckless to encourage student activists, if only by falling back before them, without providing them with analytic tools and the means for distinguishing serious objectives from self-expression. As unpleasant as activism may be for those at the receiving end, it is important to nourish the impulse to challenge established institutions and there is no better time than the time at school. And the era we were moving into in the mid-1970s increasingly called for activism.

One can reduce this paragraph to a syllogism:

a) Activism is important.
b) Activism requires tools.
c) Schools are required to provide tools for activism.

McGovern Campaign

In Washington, I had from time to time done services for Senator George McGovern—helping to draft speeches, studying welfare and food stamp programs in Virginia for his Senate Select Committee on Nutrition and Human Needs, talking on his behalf to people like Jesse Jackson and Leonard Greene about income maintenance policy. (Greene, a New York State industrialist, was urging a "Fair Share" income maintenance proposal on McGovern, who asked me to evaluate it.) Inevitably and enthusiastically, these activities merged into a role in McGovern's 1972 presidential campaign.

McGovern was committed to creating a government program to increase the cash income of poor people. This commitment derived from deep-seated convictions about social justice, much reinforced by his experiences with the so-called Hunger Committee. He was convinced that we needed a type of program which, unlike welfare, would not undermine incentive to work. Moreover, by the late 1960s work and work-and-training reforms of welfare had been tried and discredited. McGovern's belief that a new type of program was needed obviously accorded with my own convictions.

I have indicated that McGovern's trial balloons about a

children's allowance made it clear that supporting it would be damaging to a campaign; I abandoned it for the duration. The senator was surrounded by influential advisers—economists chiefly—who urged him to declare for a negative income tax. Naturally, I opposed this; this was a familiar argument for me. There were other ideas, of course. McGovern seemed not to want to get deeply involved in choosing among alternatives. He thought that staking out the need for a new program and naming possible alternatives would be adequate for campaign purposes.

By the end of 1971, however, McGovern was offering specific tax proposals (a radical increase in estate taxes, a minimum tax and an increase in corporate tax rates) and ideas about income maintenance that he tried to keep general. In order to lend reality to his discussions, he used Leonard Greene's proposal as an example: a government payment of $4,000 for every family of four, to be taxed back at the rate at which the family paid taxes. In effect, this would be a children's allowance, expanded to include adults.

"It's the only way I can figure," McGovern said, "to permit people to derive a minimum income, welfare assistance or whatever you want to call it without losing it when they go to work."[4] Cost estimates had not been prepared for this proposal, nor could they readily be prepared, so there was some confusion about what McGovern had in mind. It did not help that, as a favor to the National Welfare Rights Organization (NWRO), but without himself endorsing the bill, McGovern introduced a $6,500 minimum income plan (a negative income tax) in the United States Senate. President Nixon had proposed a $1,600 minimum—pitiful, of course, but the high NWRO figure was unreal.

There was not much media attention at first; some press reaction even credited McGovern with being innovative. In New York now and occupied with my school's problems, I was not deeply engaged until, in May 1972, I watched a televised debate in California between McGovern and Hubert Humphrey, then his principal rival for the Democratic nomination.

Humphrey treated the NWRO proposal as McGovern's. He presented extravagant cost estimates of $72 billion for the NWRO and Greene proposals. McGovern did not have his own estimates, so he had trouble disputing these. Humphrey estimated the requisite tax increase for moderate-income people and McGovern was not adequately prepared to contradict this, either. Humphrey criticized McGovern for not requiring beneficiaries to work. The debate was a debacle for McGovern. It became obvious that his proposals would have to be rethought.[5]

Home in Washington again, he named two working groups: one on taxation, chaired by Adrian De Wind, a senior partner at the Paul Weiss Rifkind law firm in New York, and one on welfare, chaired by me. McGovern was scheduled to speak to the New York Society of Securities Analysts in Wall Street on August 29, 1972, and he would present his new positions. The tax group, including such other luminaries as Stanley Surrey, Joseph Pechman and William Vickrey (respectively, a lawyer and two economists) presented a package that called for closing major tax loopholes and taxing capital gains as ordinary income. It promised $22 billion in new federal revenue. This package replaced earlier tax proposals (notably, a 77 percent inheritance tax on estates over $500,000) that had drawn considerable criticism. The tax group also supported a negative income tax.

The welfare group supported the tax proposals but otherwise went an entirely different route. We proposed expansion and improvements of social security in ways that would particularly assist poor people, extension of unemployment insurance, and a modest tax credit plan constructed like the current earned income tax credit. It was a pluralistic approach, building on existing principles and programs. We supported a public service jobs proposal that came from Nancy Amidei of McGovern's Select Committee staff; it might take as many as one million people off welfare. Except for the public service jobs component, the package would seem modest, one that he could run on without difficulty; yet, all of its provisions were useful. A fundamentally new cash program could be entertained after McGovern was president.

Virtually all the advice he received was contrary to ours, that is, in favor of a negative income tax, and was dismissive of the social security and other changes. James Tobin, not yet a Nobel laureate, worked out the details of Leonard Greene's proposal. It did, indeed, prove to be expensive and to involve taxing middle-income people, and McGovern dropped it.

At a meeting of mainly economic advisers, on a hot August day, with perhaps twenty people circled on chairs on the sun-struck, emerald green lawn of a Kennedy home in suburban Virginia, almost everyone urged a negative income tax on McGovern. Only former HEW secretary Wilbur Cohen and I—who alone, I thought, had grasped how it would work out in real life and what it would mean in a campaign—were less than enthusiastic. Beginning a statement in opposition, I said that "I may be the only one here who thinks this would be disastrous social policy and a disastrous campaign move. . . ." McGovern interrupted to say: "That you're the only one doesn't mean that you're wrong." I thought he was being kind, but the outcome suggests that he agreed.

Gordon Weil, McGovern's executive assistant, arranged a luncheon for him with Arthur Okun, Joseph Pechman and Charles Schultze—leading economists all—the day before his Wall Street speech. They intended to put to rest any doubts the senator might retain about supporting a negative income tax. By the end of the luncheon, they thought that they had. When I learned about this development, I told McGovern that I would have to withdraw from the scheduled Wall Street press confer-ence if he made such a proposal. He said that he would not.

The Wall Street speech went well. The press focused on the tax proposals. *Time* magazine credited McGovern with systematizing "questions about the equity of the tax system and the nation's spending priorities that will not fade away." And McGovern was not mired down in the kind of confused public argument that a negative income tax would have invited and that he had engaged in with Humphrey.

What had already been said nevertheless proved to be a drag on the campaign. In its aftermath, McGovern placed part of the blame for losing the election on what the public came to know as the $1,000 per person payment (derived from Greene's $4,000 for a family of four). With all the public discussion about the earlier taxation and welfare proposals, failing to settle on one set of proposals and stay with it left a sense of weakness and indecision. This appearance was compounded by the selection of U.S. Senator Thomas Eagleton as his running mate and then, following the revelation that Eagleton had been hospitalized for depression, Eagleton's withdrawal from the slate. At first, McGovern was quoted as saying that he backed Eagleton 1,000 percent; then he had to retreat from that. One thousand was not a lucky number for McGovern.

Much else was in play, of course. In 1963, McGovern had been the first senator to criticize American involvement in Vietnam, a point of view that now had a considerable following. However, Nixon was able to cloud his belligerent policy in Vietnam in various ways. As the election approached, word was spread around that peace was "at hand"—but there was no peace. Nixon was able to appear as a world statesman, opening China and arriving at disarmament and trade agreements with the Soviet Union. This was more or less while McGovern was mud-wrestling with Humphrey in California. It may be, as some of us thought afterwards, that Nixon was going to be reelected, no matter what.

With the election imminent, in October, the *Washington Post* ran a story on the financing of the Watergate burglary out of a secret $700,000 slush fund controlled by Nixon aides. McGovern observed that the "chain of scandal and corruption runs to the very heart of Mr. Nixon's White House operation."[6] However, this was before the more sensational revelations in the *Post* and the *Los Angeles Times,* and other media paid no attention.

Long after the election, De Wind wrote to me that McGovern "is a fine and dedicated man but not a 'politician' in the campaign sense."[7] De Wind points to the heart of the matter. In subsequent elections, character—bad character, that is—has increasingly become an issue. It is profoundly important to remember that McGovern had *good* character. Investigative reporters do not ferret out good character.

It boggles the mind to think how differently the last twenty years might have developed without the fruits in 1973 and 1974 of Nixon's bad character. There would not have been the paradox of bombing villages to hasten the peace process; the Watergate cover-up; the subversion of agencies like the Internal Revenue Service and Central Intelligence Agency for disinformation purposes and to punish "enemies"; the forced resignation of high officials and, in the face of impeachment, the president himself; and the three- or four-year hiatus in dealing with national needs. From Colonial times on, Americans have tended to distrust government, but generations of Americans now distrust more profoundly, our attitudes still colored by the paranoia and brutalities of that fevered and convulsed seventeen months.

NOTES

1. Nine pamphlets were published by the Center for Studies in Income Maintenance Policy, Graduate School of Social Work, New York University, in the years 1971 to 1973. They were:

   A. Winifred Bell, Robert Lekachman and Alvin L. Schorr, "Public Policy and Income Distribution."

   B. Winifred Bell and Dennis M. Bushe, "Neglecting the Many, Helping the Few: The Impact of the 1967 AFDC Work Incentives."

   C. Winifred Bell, "Family Structure and Poverty Trends: A Collision Course."

Martha N. Ozawa, "Welfare and National Economic Policy." Reprint.

"Four More Years of Welfare Nightmare." Reprint.

Alvin L. Schorr, "Welfare Reform—The Use of Words to Obscure Issues."

D. Helen Ginsburg, "Unemployment, Sub-Employment and Public Policy."

E. Helen Ginsburg, "Unemployment or Full Employment? Needed: A National Commitment to Full Employment." Reprint.

"Deliberate Unemployment: The Strategy of Misery." Reprint.

F. Martha N. Ozawa, "Taxation and Social Welfare." Reprint.

Winifred Bell, "Demogrants, Negative Income Taxes, and Tax Credits."

Alvin L. Schorr, "Tax Exemptions and Tax Credits."

G. Martha N. Ozawa, "Individual Equity versus Social Adequacy in Federal Old Age Insurance." Reprint.

"Children's Right to Economic Security." Reprint.

"SSI—Progress or Retreat." Reprint.

H. Alvin L. Schorr, "Social Services After Eden." Memorial Lecture for Richard Titmuss.

I. Rachel Floersheim Boaz, "The Burden of Medical Care."

2. For example, Martha N. Ozawa, *Income Maintenance and Work Incentives: Toward a Synthesis,* Praeger, New York, 1982.

3. Alvin L. Schorr, ed., *Jubilee for Our Times,* Columbia University Press, New York, 1977.

4. Gordon L. Weil, *The Long Shot,* W. W. Norton, New York, 1973, p. 76, pp. 79ff.

5. Ibid.

6. Richard Dougherty, *Goodbye, Mr. Christian,* Doubleday and Co., New York, 1973, p. 238.

7. Adrian De Wind, personal letter to Alvin L. Schorr, 9 December 1993.

The Community
Service Society
of New York

The Community Service Society of New York, or CSS as it is known, is an old and well-endowed social service agency that was once the favorite New York City charity of wealthy Protestants such as the Rockefellers and Astors. In its evolution from two nineteenth-century ancestors, the Association for Improving the Condition of the Poor and the Charity Organization Society,[1] CSS tracked the evolution of American social work and social improvement. By the 1950s, it was known across the country as the premier family service organization.

Through much of its long history, the Community Service Society was in the grip of the "CSS saga," a tradition that required it to be in the vanguard of professionalism and "a spearhead of community action."[2] It conducted the country's first demonstration of subsidized "model housing." It opened the first public showers: "French baths." It lobbied for a tax on ships that carried immigrants to the United States—to help support them if they became indigent. It established a professional school for social workers, now the Columbia University School of Social Work. It founded New York City's Welfare Council, later the Community Council. And on and on.

In an extensive self-study completed in 1971, the CSS board decided that family service was well established and widely understood and its usefulness need no longer be demonstrated. The board voted to phase out its family service program (drawing considerable criticism from social workers and social agencies across the country) and to adopt a more trailblazing, community-oriented, social-activist posture. As is not uncommon in such situations, the board was divided on the decision; the new policies brought in new officers, who represented the winning faction. The losers, more devoted to delivering tried social services than to social adventure, would wait for another day.

I was interviewed for the position of CSS's general director as I was leaving NYU in early 1973. Board members described the policy they planned to pursue: developing social policies and experimental social services that would reduce poverty in New York City. Bemused, I observed that CSS was embarking on War Against Poverty strategies just as the nation was leaving them behind. However, I supported such policies and would be glad to undertake the work.

I had come to think that the best indication that I should accept a job was that it was uncharted and intimidating. For this CSS position, however, my entire career could be viewed as preparation. I had been trained and worked as a caseworker. I had worked with lay boards as a family service administrator. I knew government policy from the inside out. The agency might do little that I had not dealt with and thought about. This sense of mastery had its own charm.

I first learned of my appointment when a friend, Bernard Shiffman, director of the Community Council of Greater New York, called to say he was taking me to Wallach's Men's Shop: He had learned that I was to be named general director and I would need to dress up to the position.

The agency was in disarray. Many staff members had been dismissed while others had been left without guidance. At CSS's invitation, carelessly considered, community groups had submitted perhaps a hundred proposals for CSS funding. Some proposals were rejected out of hand; they were the lucky ones, for none was approved. Without drawing a challenge, a local foundation withheld $100,000 a year that was owed to CSS, because they thought it could be used better elsewhere. Little service to clients, careless handling of funds, drift and low credibility characterized the agency inside and out.

There appeared to be three necessary tasks: to reorganize and tighten administration, to make it clear what work the agency was doing and set about doing it, and to establish credibility with clients, the social service community and our own staff. This last, I thought, should follow from completing the first two tasks.

Reorganized Administration

In the nature of CSS tradition and purposes, lay board and committee members played a central role. Over the years, this dynamic probably contributed to the agency's flexibility and capacity to change direction. Also, the status and calibre of many of these lay people, when they were engaged, made CSS a powerful voice on the New York scene. On the other hand, their deep involvement could lead to false starts and midstream shifts of direction and to uncertainty about who was responsible to whom. One result of these uncertainties, no doubt, was that, of three general directors who immediately preceded me, one had been appointed to serve until his imminent retirement and the other two had left at the board's suggestion.

At the time, the president of the board was Robert W. Sweet, a former deputy mayor of New York City; a little later he would be named a federal judge. While we were planning the reorganization, he said speculatively that perhaps this partnership of lay people and professional administrators was inefficient and even unworkable. *Maybe the general director should be president and CEO at once? The board could meet quarterly to assure that he* [that is, I] *did not steal the furniture.* Partly for the reasons indicated above, I was not inclined to go this route, nor was I sure he was serious.

The implicit choice to enhance the power or authority of the board was at the heart of our reorganization. We sought also to integrate the agency's structure, reduce layers of administration and strengthen the executive. Integrating administration meant, in particular, bringing together, in the Office of the General Director, oversight of CSS's policy function (public affairs, as it was called) and social service programs. The board's explicit decision to seek a strong executive was, in CSS's circumstances, plainly necessary.

The organizational pattern at which we arrived vested oversight in lay committees for eight subject matter areas: aging, education, social services, health, youth and corrections, housing and urban development, income security, and consumer affairs. Each committee was to be responsible for programs we operated as well as for broad policy conclusions in its subject matter area. The committees would be assisted by assigned professional staff. A board planning and research committee, served by program development and research staff, would establish agency priorities and a budget. Thus, the agency budget would reflect board decisions about agency priorities.

In due course, strains developed: From time to time, committees arrived at public affairs positions or recommendations for operating programs that were contrary to the board's own policies. The board repeatedly declined to deal with these conflicts.

One such occasion came up when the state legislature, endeavoring to protect public education in the face of New York City's financial difficulties, considered specifying the percentage of the city's budget that should be allocated to education. The board's executive committee had taken a position against municipal budgeting by formula: It would be mechanical and a way to avoid making judgments about relative need. Seeing an advantage for public education in the bill, however, the education committee asked the board whether *the committee* might support it. The board declined to discuss the matter.

In general, I found myself saying to committees that they must accept the positions of the board or its executive committee. In the process, I angered some people and made no friends. Long after, I concluded that I had expected more order and consistency than the board required or cared about.

Not infrequently, differences between committees or between a committee and the board had financial consequences. Committees would recommend studies or new programs for which there was no room in the budget. The planning and research committee, which was supposed to be the budget's guardian, tended to accept committee proposals even when they would lead to a deficit. Despite protests by the finance committee, the board also proved reluctant to deny funding to programs that had the strongly committed support of one or another board member.

An example was a casework program, the Older Person's Service, that had been carried over from earlier years. Like the family service program that had been dropped, it was a sound program, whose work was well understood and widely established. Taking my mandate seriously, I said that it would have to evolve into an experimental program or be phased out. Meanwhile, I opposed increasing its budget. The CSS committee on aging recommended additional funds and won a compromise from the planning committee, and so from the board. I got a clue to how my role was regarded when I met Ollie Randell, an old friend prominent in the field of the aging, on her way to a meeting of the committee on aging. I had not seen her in some years and her greeting was: "Hello, Alvin. I hear you're against us!"

In an effort to clarify policy, I circulated a set of criteria for new programs and weighed in against programs that did not meet them. Even so, we ran a substantial deficit from year to year. I was not entirely upset by this. Needs in the city were truly desperate; moreover, the perturbations of the stock market affected our deficit more than contested budget items. However, finance committee members were upset and, as trustees tended to be polite with one another, they blamed the general director.

Perhaps it goes without saying that staff members sometimes found themselves trapped between me and members of the committee they served or between one committee and another. It did not moderate the strain when I stipulated that every committee was required to have members who represented minorities and clients. This requirement threatened to undermine the control of both staff and current lay committee members.

Set down in just this way—with the advantage, to be sure, of knowing what happened in the next three or four years—it seems remarkable that I did not see that it was not going to work. On the other hand, we had to have a structure that would adapt itself to the bi-modal policy and service functions of the agency; to committees' insistence on being independent of the administrator and the board;[3] and to the CSS saga: the conviction that the agency (board and staff together) was first and best.

We used a variety of experienced consultants in working out the new structure. None forecast what would happen.

Operating Social Service Programs

It was to be a year or two before the strains would really manifest themselves. Meanwhile, we planned new service programs with relevant lay committees and launched them. These had to meet the test of being either genuinely experimental or serving public policy purposes. By the time I left four years later, we had dozens of operating programs. Staff members saw ten thousand clients—each on five separate occasions, on average—during the year. In addition, we held over eleven thousand group meetings. A few words will have to suffice to describe five of these programs.

Natural Support Program   Under pressure from me, the Older Persons Service, a conventional counseling service, was reformulated to focus on the family relationships of older people, in particular the help that is provided by family members, friends and neighbors. Experimental mutual support groups were organized in four boroughs of the city for the people who *give* care: "caregivers." Much was learned about how families, friends and neighbors connect with elderly people and what may usefully be done to ease the burden of caregivers; for some elderly people, nursing home care was avoided or postponed; and a great many were helped by techniques that had not until then been taken seriously or well understood: for example, mutual support, counseling focused on their burdens, respite arrangements.[4]

By the end of a four-year experimental period, dozens of presentations had been offered at professional meetings; articles, books and manuals had been published. CSS went on to test with families of disabled people the techniques that had been developed in work with the elderly. Similar programs are being launched twenty years later—a result for which we earnestly wished—and are still being described as innovations. Well after I had left the agency, in 1981, in what I took to be a gesture of reconciliation, I was invited to address a CSS celebration reporting on the successes of the program.

ACCESS ACCESS, touched on in Chapter 4, was a program for families that had improperly been denied welfare. If we decided that they were in fact strictly eligible, we helped establish that fact with the city's Human Resources Administration (HRA). Meanwhile, as the judgment that they were eligible meant that they were seriously needy, we provided cash assistance at welfare levels. For a while, forty to fifty families a day would apply to our office in East (Spanish) Harlem (not all of whom proved to be legally eligible, of course). With living costs rising while, simultaneously, welfare was being cut back in curious and imaginative ways, the number applying to us climbed rapidly to two hundred a day. A goodly number *were* eligible, as HRA eventually had to conclude. It was a dramatic indication of the extent of stark need in New York City and of the failure of HRA to perform its work in accordance with law.

Publicizing what we learned led HRA to examine its own

processes. Finding that 50 percent of denials were made in error, HRA instituted reforms. With respect to welfare, however, reforms of this sort evaporate as soon as one looks away. In the climate that was current, enforcing strict adherence to law by welfare agencies required unremitting effort, which we tried to sustain.

Technical Assistance   In 1975, the City of New York revised its charter to turn over considerable official responsibility to local community boards. CSS had strongly supported such a move, conducting charter workshops and distributing a guide to the proposed charter revisions in English, Spanish and Chinese. Once enacted, the Technical Assistance Office of CSS conducted a series of seminars in Manhattan and the Bronx to help current and potential members of community boards to carry out their new role. In Brooklyn and Queens, seminars were conducted on how to evaluate city services and how to make budget decisions. Besides preparing community board members for their work, these meetings helped to maintain the momentum of decentralization.

The new charter provisions were scheduled to go into effect January 1, 1977. When the city appeared to be dragging its feet on implementation, CSS called a press conference. We asked that the city dismantle its Office of Neighborhood Services, which would now duplicate community board functions, and transfer its $3 million annual budget to the new boards. We also asked that the city issue guidelines for selecting community board members and clarify how it would report city expenditures in each community district.

One effect of our preparatory work was that community board members trusted CSS staff and engaged us in working out problems as they developed. As needs became evident, Technical Assistance staff prepared written materials for the boards, codifying responsibilities and ways of proceeding.

The director who led this office, Ellen Lurie, was a talented and experienced community organizer. Intense and impatient, she was quickly frustrated by what she regarded as the elitism and conservatism of CSS—me included, or maybe me most of all. At one point, she came to see me to proffer her resignation. When I said she was resigning because she was afraid of failure, it made her so angry that she withdrew the resignation. Lurie became increasingly frustrated, she made it plain to me, but under her leadership her office did important work. Despite a strained relationship, I was fond of her and believe that she was fond of me. She became ill and died not long after I left and, very appropriately, CSS established an annual award honoring her.

Single-Parent Family Center The center started with a drop-in storefront, where child care was provided while single parents talked to one another, gathered information, and gained some sense that they were not alone with their problems. We learned that the most precious commodity that single parents lack is *time*. Thus, we had to be weaned from the idea that they would turn up according to schedule. The center experimented with filling important niches—open and welcoming on holidays such as Christmas, and offering a specially organized summer camp session for children and mothers. With a consultant architect, Louis Sauer, and sociologist John Zeisel we studied whether more suitable housing designs can be devised for single-parent families than apartments typically modeled on our grandparents' homes (although the descendants of those designs are smaller and have more technology). Indeed, there seem to be.[5] We explored the idea of building or converting housing to designs more functional for single parents, but it did not come off.

In time, the CSS Center—like the Natural Supports Program, one of the very first in the country—became an independent, self-sustaining agency. It went on to new experiments, such as special arrangements for imprisoned mothers to care for their own young children and providing special services for homeless one-parent families. I had a hope—not to be realized—that the center would join with other, similar groups springing up

across the country to form a national single-parent family organization, as had happened in Britain and France. Setting
aside Parents Without Partners, which is largely social and
middle class, such an organization has never developed here.

Ultimately, I concluded that the American approach to
single parents tends to be psychological: coaching parents how
to teach their children, providing group support, enhancing
self-esteem. Such inward-looking approaches do not lend
themselves to regional or national organizing agendas. By contrast, European programs for single-parent groups are heavily
economic and provide a common meeting ground on such
issues as welfare levels and working conditions.

CAUSE   In their nature, not all experiments succeed. It
has to be judged that CAUSE (Community Association United
in Services for Everyone—a mouthful never to be spoken) was
one that did not succeed. We learned a lesson that everyone in
the business already knew intuitively; even so, learning by way
of a serious trial was useful.

A universal problem of local social services is that they
overlap, compete for attention, pass people around. It is virtually impossible to make sense of their pattern. They waste large
amounts of money and clients' time and energy in fending off
and referring cases. Solutions that pop up regularly, such as
information centers and grouping services under one roof, may
compound rather than ease the problem.

At CSS, we thought it probably less important to integrate
locations than to integrate functions. Structural innovation
would be required. We would rely on two principles that had,
to our knowledge, never been tried: Services brought together
would *be responsible to a single administrator* and there would be
no duplication in work done. Once a staff member had heard a
problem or verified some criterion of eligibility (age, need,
whatever), clients would not be expected to repeat this process.
For example, a caseworker who had dealt with a client about
day care—and verified the client's financial circumstances—

would not need to go through another verification procedure if the client applied for welfare. This kind of mechanical repetition happens widely, of course.

With a degree of hubris, no doubt, we thought that with our influence and a considerable investment of money ($500,000 a year), we might bring service integration off. After exploration and encouragement from neighborhood residents and what would be the major players—the Human Resources Administration, in particular—we established CAUSE in Chelsea, on the west side of downtown New York. CAUSE was to be a neighborhood-based integrated service center. Area residents seeking assistance with personal or family matters would find there a wide range of services: family counseling, child welfare service, and income maintenance. They might register for summer camp. They might be trained for volunteer activities—in Spanish if they liked. They could (and did) organize a rent strike. They might attend a health clinic.

Organizing and staffing the service was the least of our problems. Enormous effort went into securing participation by HRA, despite the interest and sympathy of three successive HRA administrators. In CAUSE's first year, we chronicled sixteen separate top-level conferences with HRA. We searched for a formula that would allow a Chelsea center worker to take an application for public assistance. Each of several proposals to assure last-word review and decision by HRA was judged to violate regulations or law, and HRA would not join us in seeking a waiver of regulations or a change in law.

Other agencies that served the neighborhood participated in various ways and, a survey revealed, appreciated "CAUSE's outreach, community planning, broad range of services, and generalist approach." Two years into the project, however, our evaluation staff predicted that the project would not be successful because of "the imperialistic and boundary setting characteristics of organizations, and organization and professional emphasis upon specialized rather than generalized practice."[6]

In no event were social agencies willing to have their staff members answer to an outside administrator.

So our first lesson was what everyone had always known: Fragmentation may have developed for reasons of history and complexity but, once established, it is reinforced by institutional interest. We could not beat it. Another lesson might be drawn: We would not see the integration of services unless and until such a pattern was imposed by funding sources.

During this period, as part of an anniversary celebration, CSS staged an international seminar on integration of social services. The keynote address was delivered by Frederic Lord Seebohm. He was chairman of Barclays Bank International; ten years before the conference he had presided over a highly successful reorganization of British social services.[7] Thus, he had sterling credentials that would impress any audience we might assemble. I knew quite well that his address would be a reasoned, humane, businesslike argument for integrated services. Lay and professional leadership of American social services and representatives from other countries heard him speak and then spent two days discussing integrated services.

Later, two professors who had been participants, Alfred J. Kahn and Sheila Kamerman, both at Columbia University, led a nationwide effort to establish integrated social service departments. They were encouraged and funded by HEW. They did a good deal of work and generated much interest and excitement, but this broader effort was not to take hold.

I thought I heard its death knell when an assistant secretary at HEW, Arabella Martinez, said in a speech ostensibly supporting these projects that diversity must flourish. Having established an escape hatch, Martinez was not prepared to use HEW's funding power to press for participation. In any event, the special interests that would oppose service integration—mental health, disability, child welfare, and all the rest—were already too powerful. By contrast, Britain had established a rational social services structure well before special interests became entrenched.

Public Affairs

Public policy activities were centered in CSS's eight subject-matter lay committees, each chaired by a board member. Upwards of two hundred and fifty lay people, many of them expert in their committee's subject matter, were involved. The committees worked closely with research and evaluation staff, so that deliberations and position statements were commonly based on staff research. As the committees had authority over operating social service programs as well, their agendas and their findings often sensitively reflected what was learned in these programs.

Thus, a *New York Times* report of a study showing that welfare recipients were well off was accompanied by a same-day, same-page rebuttal based on our experience with ACCESS. A CSS study of experiments to control health care costs in twenty-two states and Canada led us to advocate a system of "prospective reimbursement" for hospitals. In time, the government adopted prospective reimbursement (or Diagnostic Related Groups—DRGs) as a payment system for Medicare.

It is difficult, in a few words, to convey the range and authority of material that came from these research studies and deliberations. When I reflect on this, I am struck anew by the imagination, devotion and unpretentious moral courage of these lay people and staff members. It would be unconscionable to have failed to use their work to fullest effect.

Some further examples: Reports were produced on the problems of the family courts, on bilingual education, and (from a field study) on homeless youths. City enforcement of housing codes was surveyed, and recommendations offered. When the city cut back on day care for children, the effects on families were studied and duly reported; and a better, less expensive program was recommended. A report was developed on the pricing of prescription drugs. Two studies showed that a state law requiring reports of child abuse had the perverse effect, in the absence of additional funding, of diverting treatment staff to investigations.

We maintained a staff member in Albany during the state legislative session, and other staff traveled back and forth. At the end of the 1975 session, we recorded these results: "Passed, a bill providing financial assistance for aged and disabled people in emergencies. Vetoed, a bill opposed by CSS that would have expanded contracting-out to private concerns of busing handicapped children to school. Near passage (we will have another go at it), a bill mandating statewide participation in federal school food programs. Passed, four out of five bills proposed by CSS on the basis of its studies of Small Claims Court. Passed (after seven lean and hard-working years), a bill providing that landlords, in renting a dwelling, warrant it to be habitable. Passed, Prisoner's Rights legislation."[8]

After I had been at CSS about a year, a trustee who had quickly become a friend, Robert S. Potter, introduced a resolution that "the extent of income inequality" be recognized as a major concern of CSS. There ensued three or four months of sometimes heated study and debate about income inequality. At one point in a board meeting, when I was illustrating how tax policy affected income distribution, Herbert P. Patterson, formerly chairman of the board at Chase Manhattan Bank, said drily: "Listen, Alvin, that's my money you're talking about."

I would not have chosen to get into an argument about income inequality just then; too much was going on and I thought we did not need the resolution to pursue the policies we were pursuing. So I asked Potter why he did. "Well," he said cheerfully, "before we hired you, I read everything you wrote." In the end, the board approved the resolution by a large majority. In the process the board did, as a matter of fact, expand the scope of the agency's work—to include employment and tax policies. A couple of years later we produced a set of "Recommendations for a More Equitable Real Estate Tax System." And CSS began work on employment issues, ultimately producing a report in 1983 on ". . . a Program for Full Employment in New York."

I was intrigued by the board's decision to try to reduce income inequality. Over the long course of CSS's history, shipowners had joined in recommendations to tax themselves and high corporate officers had supported Medicare when it was widely said to represent socialism. And now, despite his protest, Patterson voted *for* the "income inequality" resolution. I wondered and sometimes asked but could never satisfy myself that I understood what it was about CSS that repeatedly led its lay people to support policies as a board that many would never have been heard to support individually.

Occasionally, I had a substantial difference with committee members. Earlier, I mentioned my disappointment on finding that CSS was providing social services in the Diego-Beekman housing rehabilitation project in the south Bronx. I had learned from bitter experience that social services do not compensate for a basically unviable neighborhood economy or for a vacuum of basic services such as police and trash collection.

In due course, CSS research and evaluation staff brought to the housing committee a critical evaluation of the Diego-Beekman project, indicating that it was not working out well and that the CSS contribution had achieved little.[9] The membership of the committee was chiefly socially concerned officers of banks and savings and loan associations (not yet a term of opprobrium). The committee would not approve publication of the report.

In vain, I urged the committee to consider that negative findings could be useful, too, and that a defensive posture with respect to the agency's programs would make it impossible to get true evaluations done.[10] They had signed on because they believed in the agency's purposes and programs and they were not about to undermine them. Nor could they understand how I, a committed social worker, could propose to do so. However, they did not object when, later, I was invited to testify about neighborhood rehabilitation to the banking committee of the

U.S. House of Representatives and undertook to tell the Diego-Beekman story, as I saw it.

Another difference of opinion concerned a budget and credit counseling service (BUCCS), to be run chiefly by volunteers, which a group of lay people wanted to establish. After consulting staff, I said I thought it not sufficiently experimental and would not support it. The proponents fought for their proposal, taking it through the committee process and on to the board. The board supported it; the program was established and became successful. It developed its own funding and became independent; it was copied; and banks and consumer organizations showed much interest in what could be learned from its experience.

In the overall flow of work, such differences on particular issues were exceptional and might have been expected. Nonetheless, some disagreements—BUCCS, in particular—left lay people, including some trustees, resentful. They said I always insisted on having my own way; in these two instances, at any rate, I did not have my own way.

Overall, our public affairs work showed focus and creativity. In a difficult climate (reaction against the War Against Poverty, against Vietnam and the student movement, cynicism born of Watergate, and weariness about civil rights) and in the midst of New York City's threatened bankruptcy, we took arms against the city's sea of troubles. We recorded some successes, and it may be fair to say that we helped in at least some measure to stem the tide of reaction.

The Trustees and I: The End Game

CSS's 125th anniversary celebration, almost two years into my four-year tenure, was probably the high point of my relations with the board of directors. I had helped Lord Frederic Seebohm as a consultant to his Committee on British Social Services, and now he gracefully returned the favor. During the introduction to his speech to our international seminar on integrated social services, he wondered aloud why he had crossed the Atlantic to talk about the British reorganization. "Why," he answered himself, "Alvin asked me and so I had to come."

We had arranged to give CSS's Award for Distinguished Humanitarian Service to Alva and Gunnar Myrdal at our festive anniversary dinner. Just the day before the dinner, the Nobel Committee announced that it would confer the award in economics on Gunnar Myrdal. Thus, an affair that would have attracted only local media drew national media as well. Accepting the Humanitarian Award for both of them, Alva Myrdal, herself a distinguished sociologist and ambassador, delivered an address on reducing income inequality.

Amidst the parties and receptions and media attention, everything that was said and written affirmed CSS's history and its current direction. It took a little while to recover from the glow of all this. Nevertheless, within a few months I was meeting over a cup of coffee with a couple of friends for a reality check.

It seemed plain that a number of board members were aggrieved in a way that would persist and, in tacit alliance with perhaps half a dozen well-placed, disaffected staff members (out of more than three hundred), would create considerable mischief. The nature of the complaints, at least as they were voiced, was almost entirely personal—that I was arrogant, insensitive, unyielding. I felt at least the first two complaints to be wholly unfair but, once lodged, dealing with them was like trying to prove a negative.

Privately, I concluded that I had between one and two years to stabilize the agency's programs and systems in ways that could be passed on. Several people advised me to spend more time in private conversations with trustees. A compliment was buried in this advice: If trustees really came to know me, they would dismiss the accusations. I agreed to try to arrange more informal conversations than would occur in the normal course of events. These proved fascinating but changed little, I thought.

For example, I asked to see Margaret Burden. Peggy, as everyone called her, was a wealthy woman (it was said that she would bequeath $1 million to CSS) who had a solid position in New York City society. She was particularly important because three or four of the younger women board members seemed eager to please her. Peggy was committed to delivering tried social services, for the elderly in particular; I understood that these commitments meant that I had two strikes against me.

We had a drink or two in the mellow light in one corner of her large, decorous living room. A breathtaking bronze Brancusi in the foyer and a Tinguely and a small Renoir on the walls, I remember, lent a civilized background murmur to our conversation. Burden was gracious; we talked about time she had spent abroad and about social services that interested her; and a measure of warmth seemed to develop. It was getting a little late and I said, "Tell me, Peggy, you seem to have a problem with me. Is it that you think I am radical?" She said, "No, I don't think you're radical. I think you're a Marxist." And so it was truly time to go.

By May 1976, the board decided to meet in executive session without me. Douglas Williams, now president of the board, possibly not eager to deliver the message in person, sent me a letter summarizing their complaints and left for the country. The litany was familiar by now: *arrogant, devious and petty, insensitive;* and *centralization of authority. Staff morale was low* and I was "motivated by self-promotion to the damage of the Society."

Of all these complaints, it was accurate that I had centralized authority. Given the agency's structural problems and the circumstances in which I had found it, this had seemed to be the soundest course. I think it was not objectively true that morale was low, although there is always a question of "compared with what?" With what it had been before I came? With what it would be if my dismissal did not seem imminent?

Acting cautiously and all but unanimously, the executive committee of the board now affirmed, 7 to 1, its support for me, affirmed that CSS had made "substantial strides" since I came, and reaffirmed the need for a strong executive. It appointed a small committee to work closely with me to "mitigate present and future problems." In the course of several meetings, we found substantial agreement and agreed on a number of administrative and other changes.

I named a deputy general director, Charles Langdon. I had elected not to have a deputy in my first years, wanting to stay close to the establishment of new programs. Now, I was glad to do so, and trustees and staff believed that this buffer position would somewhat diffuse confrontations over specific issues. Given more time, it might well have done so.

We held a retreat for staff and lay members and developed a manual for trustees, staff and volunteers. I undertook to circulate a brief, confidential monthly letter to trustees. And so on. And I replaced a department head who, despite several warnings, continually intrigued for my discharge.

Nevertheless, matters now moved very rapidly. Votes for my dismissal had been accumulating for very different reasons: the trustees who resented me for representing, by my appointment, the faction of the board that had overthrown them; the trustees who were wedded to delivering conventional social services; the trustees who opposed budget deficits and held me responsible for them; the trustees who were angered when I failed to support a new program that interested them; and the trustees who were close to long-time staff members I had injured by dismissal or otherwise. (There were, perhaps, three or four of these, in all.)

Ironically, still another source of votes for dismissal arose from my efforts to democratize board processes. Patterson wrote to me later to thank me, among other things, for my efforts to "transform [CSS] from a 'Park Avenue-liberal' Board of Trustees to one that was representative of the wide range of constituents that CSS was trying to serve." There were one or two minority members on the board when I came. Thereafter, every nominating committee was offered the names of minority candidates; by the time I left, nine were trustees. They appeared to believe that it was time that CSS have a black general director; and that one would be named if I left.

I suggested to David Dinkins, a trustee and at the time New York's city clerk, that hints being dropped to that effect were bait: If minority trustees voted for my dismissal, in the end they would be double-crossed. I also suggested that he review what had been done for minorities during my tenure. Still, most of the minority members voted for dismissal. Some months later, I ran into a Hispanic trustee in the street, and she tearfully acknowledged and apologized for her vote. She said she had been heavily pressured.

A great deal of organizational energy was devoted to getting me dismissed: telephone calls, conversations on social occasions, small meetings. A trustee who had resigned when I came was reelected to the board, explicitly, I thought, to provide leadership for the anti-Schorr faction.

At a penultimate and then final board meeting in January 1977, charges were made and I tried to respond—briefly, because everything had already been said. A new board member, W. James Tozer, Jr., then an officer at Citibank, seemed puzzled. He had never seen a CEO under fire without hearing anything at all about the actual business of the organization. *Was the work going well or poorly?* I said a few words about services modern in conception and vital in execution. Hoping to catch the attention of finance committee members, I noted that, when I came, non-program expenditures had represented 24 percent of the budget; they now represented 12 percent. And I said that some of the problems that troubled us all were inherent in such a complex, driven organization.

The board received a memo, quite unprompted by me, signed by all eight senior members of the executive staff. It said that "substantial progress" had been made in recent months in working out difficulties and urged the trustees to reaffirm their confidence in me and let the staff get on with the important work of the Society.

The vote to dismiss was 18 to 15. Considering all the effort and the interests that were marshaled to produce this vote, the narrow margin was a moral victory—if I had been disposed to think of moral victories.

The dismissal was painful: The directorship was a lovely job for me, and I did not like losing. Still, I did not feel that the strategies that we had pursued were unsound or that I had compromised my integrity. Nor was I left to feel alone. A number of trustees were almost as upset as I. I recall in particular the distress of my good friend, Mitchell Ginsberg, and of that "neat" gentlelady, Marian Heiskell, who chaired the board. Two people wrote passionate letters of protest from hospital beds. In his letter, Herbert Patterson added:

> The role of General Director would seem to call for the patience of Job, the political acumen of a Lyndon Johnson, the personal charm of a Valentino, and the saintliness of J. C. Such a combination you ain't.[11]

The executive who followed me, Bertram M. Beck, was a widely known and experienced administrator who had for many years had a cordial relationship with his board at Henry Street Settlement. He, too, would later be asked to leave—though, with eight years' tenure, he did better than I. He was followed by David Jones—at last, a black—who has already, at this writing, served longer than any recent general director. He should teach survival techniques.

What did I learn? I learned, if I did not already know, that, like all human relationships, administration is an exchange relationship. One gives and is given to. I could well have taken pains to satisfy trustees (and staff as well) on matters that would have cost me or CSS little. Friends tried to tell me this, but it felt like bribery and I would not stoop to it. I do not think it would have changed the outcome. The dynamics inherent in the structure of CSS, especially in the relationship of its lay committees to staff and in the ambiguous authority of its lay board and committees, built up subterranean pressure which, like a volcano erupting, at times ejected a few boulders and at other times changed the countryside.

It is hard to believe that all the activity directed to ousting me was occasioned by my lack of sensitivity or gentility. The central impulse, I concluded, was to engineer a conservative counter-coup to the board's reformist coup five years earlier. Determined to get a less radical (as they saw it) general director, who would not be so single-minded about fulfilling the CSS saga, the counter-reformers saw the opportunity to enlist trustees who would vote with them for other reasons. As it seems to me, the other reasons included personal grievances, ambition for social advancement, class differences about the objectives of CSS, other policy differences, and opportunities that my departure might open up.

No day is wholly lost that produces a good line. Some months later, at a formal dinner, I came off a receiving line to find myself face to face with two CSS trustees. One had repeatedly offered to befriend me but I had never trusted him— wisely, it turned out. Detecting a certain hesitation, the other gestured at his companion and said, "Of course, you know Franco?" *"Yes,"* I said. Discerning a certain coldness, he added, "I know he is prickly." *"A little short of that,"* I said, and moved on.

A DECALOGUE

During the seven years I spent at NYU and CSS, I sometimes distilled lessons in a few words. Strung end to end, they constitute a decalogue for reformers:

I. Training does not make jobs. Job vacancies make jobs.

II. Evil people have been known to do good, and good people can do ill.

III. Power is not commonly given or devolved; it must be taken.

IV. Doing good often advertises itself as doing good. So does doing bad. It is a problem.

V. Do not be consumed by ends; neither should you think only of means.

VI. A good planning process may not affect policy. Follow the man or woman who knows when it can or will.

VII. In a land of checker players, the chess player may lose.

VIII. Unfortunately, it often works better to be wrong at the right time than to be right at the wrong time.

IX. Public and social services are not put there to secure the interests of their staffs or boards. They are put in place for the interests of clients or consumers.

Corollary: In planning and especially in reorganizing, it is easier to care about the people one sees, that is, about employees, but the task of a social agency is to care above all about the thousands one never meets, that is, about clients.

X. The reason that we do not learn from history is that we think we are smarter. And oh, we need to be!

XI. Reforms are often overdetermined: In a good cause, redundancy may be necessary.

In a decalogue for reformers, No. XI is not redundant.

NOTES

1. Of the two organizations that would merge, AICP is said to have been the wealthy one and COS the highly professional organization. In discussions of merger in 1939, the question of a new name came up. Edward Streeter suggested that the new agency be called the Association to Improve the Condition of the Poor Charity Organization Society. Clare M. Tousley, *Letter to Jeanie,* Community Service Society, 1974.

2. Gertrude S. Goldberg, "New Directions for the Community Service Society of New York: A Study of Organizational Change," *Social Service Review,* June 1980, pp. 184–219. A fuller statement may be found in Gertrude S. Goldberg, *New Directions for the Community Service Society: A Study of Organizational Change,* D.S.W. dissertation, Columbia University, New York, 1976.

3. Ibid, p. 208.

4. Anna H. Zimmer and M. Joanna Mellor, "Caregivers Make the Difference," Community Service Society, September 1981. Unpublished. Also, Joanna Mellor and George S. Getzel, "Stress and Service Needs of Those Who Care for the Aged," paper presented to the Thirty-Third Annual Scientific Meeting of the Gerontological Society, San Diego, 23 November 1980. Mimeographed.

5. Thelma Stackhouse, "Providing Housing for One Parent Families—Two Programs," Community Service Society, 1975. Unpublished.

6. Memorandum to CSS Staff from Harvey Newman, 5 November 1976, citing on p. 4 the "Interim Report on CAUSE, #6," Office of Program Planning and Review, Community Service Society, 30 May 1975.

7. For a view of the personal social service departments twenty-five years afterward, see Alvin L. Schorr, *The Personal Social Services: An Outside View,* Joseph Rowntree Foundation, York, U.K., July 1992.

8. Alvin L. Schorr, Memorandum to CSS Trustees, Committee Members, and Staff, Community Service Society, New York, 3 September 1975.

9. *Diego-Beekman Housing Project,* A Report on a Community Service Society Social Service Program in a Rehabilitated Housing Project in the South Bronx, Office of Program Planning and Research, Community Service Society, New York, September 1974. Unpublished.

10. A commentary on the perils of doing evaluation research on the agency in which one is lodged may be found in Dwight L. Frankfather, "Welfare Entrepreneurialism and the Politics of Innovation," *Social Service Review,* March 1981, pp. 129–46.

11. Herbert P. Patterson, personal letter to Alvin L. Schorr, 3 February 1977.

Limits of Reason

Throughout my career, I exhibited a measure of what has to be called naiveté—less later than earlier. At first, I approached problems as if their solutions were open and rational. If we knew the circumstances of socially orphaned children—children who lacked a parent because their parents had separated or never married at all—we might know what to do for them. If we knew what old people need and want from their children, we might know how to support children in giving it. Increasingly, however, I found myself mixing such evaluation with questions of values and ulterior motive. If American policy is not in general a pursuit of family integrity, why not? And why do we pretend that it is?

For a while, I earnestly tried to answer such questions. In a 1962 article called "Beyond Pluck and Luck,"[1] for example, I tried to account for the persistence of laws about children's responsibility to support their parents despite the patent undesirability of such laws. The article discussed widespread, powerful anxieties about the deterioration of American families, and tried to put them to rest. Applying a Freudian technique to social policy, I imagined that irrational behavior might be made to go away by exposing its sources.

After a time, it occurred to me that this, too, was naive, that particular policies, even if they seemed not important objectively, were symbols that packed great emotional weight and could exercise powerful political pull. In the 1990s, the truth of this observation is all too readily observable, of course. Fracases about the handling of the national flag and a moment of silent prayer in school may be examples. Although I took a hand from time to time at trying to shape symbols and maneuver politically, I remained at the core a policy analyst, an advocate and a rationalist—with a strong humanitarian drive, to be sure.

I was influenced by a conversation with E. Franklin Frazier in his tiny, overcrowded, overflowing-with-books-and-papers Howard University office. He was a distinguished sociologist, black, who quite early had criticized the black middle class for abandoning their poor.[2] Middle-class blacks were conceivably instructed by his criticism but were not charmed. Frazier seemed to carry a profound sense of disappointment about the failure of blacks and his university, in particular, to honor him. Yet he would not recede from naming unpleasant truths when he saw them. Acrid honesty was a barrier to the appreciation he would have liked and at the same time the core of his duty and honor.

I found myself tending in an analogous manner to deal with unpleasant truths by naming them. This meant standing up to them even if I could not change them. In the second chapter, I referred to Jewish marginality. Recently, I came upon this quotation: "When Dr. Sigmund Freud in Vienna found himself virtually ostracized for his professional insights he proudly said, 'Being a Jew, I knew I would be in the opposition.' "[3] Many Jews behave otherwise, of course; to some degree, one takes from one's culture what one chooses.

Still, as I set all this down, I am astonished at how much I was permitted, how much I participated in, and how much I got done. Accident placed me in the right places at the right time. If I had been in Pittsburgh or Peoria, where in fact I had entertained job offers, my career might have been quite different. It seems clear to me that the opportunities shaped my mind as well as the other way around.

Social Science and Public Policy

I began by looking for solutions, only to stumble upon problems. One problem was a lack of fit between social science research and issues of social policy. So many questions bearing on policy had barely been addressed.

Lack of Fit   Was it said that welfare tended to break up families? In 1959, researchers had not explored the matter. By 1965, it was widely asserted that welfare did indeed have this effect but little more research had been done. Finally, by the 1970s, social scientists were giving the question careful attention. The evidence provided no indication that welfare tends to break up families.[4] Conceivably, the situation has altered in the last twenty years, given deepening poverty and the progressive degradation of jobs, but too many social scientists still speak from old research or from conventional wisdom, which never changed, anyway.

For all the talk about single parents, there has been precious little looking at the daily experience of women (and men) with spouselessness. Everything seems to be statistics and correlations, and there is little intimate observation. And for all the talk about work and welfare, little close attention has been paid to welfare mothers' actual experience in preparing for and seeking work.[5]

Again, what are the environmental and social conditions that produce premature childbirth and, in turn, low birth weight and infant mortality? Although environmental and social conditions are certainly implicated in this sequence of problems, very little has been worked out about how.[6] As a final example of what is not studied, why is there so little exploration of how malnutrition, poor housing and sleep deprivation may be linked to passivity, low motivation and "present-orientation?"

The gaps in research hold more mystery than the work that is in process. What is being done must reflect the direction of social movement; what fails to be done, what *we do not do*, may be what we are satisfied not to know.

If one considers these research gaps, it may be evident that they exclude a number of stereotypes from examination and avoid the link between biological needs and social behavior. I have concluded that the gaps permit us to dwell on "the culture of poverty" and "the underclass"—pop-sociology scapegoats, in usage, if not in origin—that are comforting to middle-class people. Not really knowing the attitudinal and behavioral effects of physical deprivation excuses our failure to do the expensive, physical things: feed poor children adequately and build low-cost housing. Finally, more deeply, I have wondered if we are so estranged from sensuousness and the physical world (a strange thing to say these days, to be sure) that we deny their significance for poor people and, by extension, for ourselves.

Why Social Science Fails   There are many reasons why social science fails to inform policy and to challenge it when it is vulnerable. These certainly include the extent to which, because of real or potential government funding, research is dominated by the government's needs and definitions; and the extent to which academic programs, in their push for scholarly rigor, teach students to abandon unlearned common sense and to overvalue the complex and technical. I add two reasons that have troubled me over many years.

A Narrow View   One is that social scientists take a narrow view of problems that require a broader view. This is a common enough observation; Erving Goffman, a seminal sociologist, called it "trained incompetence."[7] For illustration, I offer examples of the blinkered use of two handy-dandy economists' terms: cost-effectiveness and incentives. The following are egregious examples of tunnel vision, but not different in quality from many analyses that pass as sensible.

A United Nations group was interested in the cost-effectiveness of various approaches to crime and delinquency—e.g., dollar for dollar, is prevention more effective than jails? At one point, they turned to the most cost-effective approach to preventing juvenile delinquency in Vietnam. As this did not lend itself to quantitative analysis, the relationship of juvenile delinquency to the war that was under way was not questioned or mentioned in the report![8]

Incentives were discussed in a Ford Foundation critique of America's social welfare system called "The Common Good —Social Welfare and the American Future." Published in 1989 with the imprimatur of a prestigious advisory panel, it had taken over three years to prepare, at a cost of $3 million. Yet, the report featured several careless applications of incentives, of which the following is possibly the most flagrant:

> The wonders of modern technology [the report says] may lead to a social policy dilemma: We are increasingly able to save the lives of even the smallest newborns (i.e., 1½ pounds). We want people in all situations, including but not limited to the poor, to be able to avail themselves of lifesaving technologies, but *we do not want these technologies to encourage the social behavior that triggers their use.*[9] [emphasis supplied]

That is, poor, pregnant women may eat badly, fail to see a physician and use crack *because* they count on modern technology to save their unborn child. One writes such a thing, under the banner of economic theory, having consulted no other discipline and, indeed, having no evidence of any sort, only if one is intoxicated with cant and feels free to say anything at all about stigmatized people. In discussing common people one uses vulgar theory—naturally!

An Accommodationist View   Another reason that studies fail to challenge vulnerable policy is that they so often take on the coloration of the government's policy or of the policy towards which public opinion is leaning. Over the years, for example, the Manpower Development Research Corporation (MDRC), a private research organization, has been central to the evaluation of welfare-related training for work. One MDRC study after another scrupulously reported only marginal gains from these efforts. However, casual readers (e.g, legislators and reporters) have taken encouragement about these projects from the prefaces and press releases that accompanied the reports, which were delicately slanted toward optimism, as it seems to me.

A possibly more serious and less subjective criticism may be arrived at by reviewing the outcomes that MDRC chose to study: whether job training helps women on welfare find jobs, whether they keep them very long, whether they increase their overall income, whether they go off assistance, and whether the government saves money in the end. Although there is indirect evidence that many children receive poorer care when their mothers enroll in these projects and, indeed, are more poorly nourished (because of cash penalties that are applied),[10] no question was asked about such outcomes. If such outcomes were collected and reported, however, their negative weight might swamp positive but marginal findings about improvements in the trainees' income.

What is one to make of this? It seems evident that many researchers are not solely observers and analysts of the social scene but are carried along by it. They may speak a more disciplined and guarded language but they ride the waves of political will and popular opinion.

I have now made a contribution to an old argument. In their work, social scientists generally claim to be value-free. As far back as 1939, however, sociologist Robert Lynd wrote that, in framing questions for investigation, the social scientist "tacitly [accepts] the inclusive value judgment of the culture as to the . . . need for only minor remedial changes."[11] Research, he said, should center instead on social needs. Almost thirty years later, sociologist Howard Becker made a similar observation.[12] And the accounts about cost analysis and incentives above, another thirty years along, illustrate the same point.

The (self-deluded) claim of a value-free orientation is a hardy weed, disappearing under attack and then returning to take over the field again. Under the cover of a value-free orientation, social science goes with the dominant mood.

In these days of incessant talk about family values and moral values, the term "value-free" is not much in currency; researchers speak instead of being technicians or methodologists, that is, objective. Thus, they evade taking responsibility for the purposes of research and how its questions are selected.

An example of such evasion is a National Institute of Mental Health-sponsored review of "the current status of research and research training throughout the profession of social work."[13] The report that was developed notes that social work research developed out of turn-of-the-century inquiries into the causes of broad social problems and the underlying human conditions with which social workers deal. Without transition, it goes on to observe that "today" (in the face of epidemic poverty, pain and conflict, today!) the more important need is for methodologists who are better trained in program effectiveness, i.e., what social work does that works.

A reviewer pointed out that the report would have been quite different "if the task force [had] focused on revealing how social institutions and cultural practices perpetuate injustice. . . ."[14] (After all, this would have honored the origins of social work research.) The report appeared not to recognize that a value choice was being made between what is important to professionals and what is important to their clientele. Thus is research led by technicians, not by intellectuals reflecting on their role and assessing the overriding social need.

In appraising these judgments, it is important to distinguish the points at which research may be value-oriented. First, values are never absent when a research question is selected. In fact, the choice of question may be and frequently is bought and paid for. Second, even so, social scientists have to be objective in designing and conducting research, including the formulation of research questions: This is the heart of the matter. Third, recommendations flowing from research certainly involve values, but at that point readers should be in a position to judge for themselves whether the findings compel the conclusions.

To review, when I entered upon policy work there was less research than now and certainly less devoted to issues bearing upon social policy. Such research was not regarded as scholarly and was not especially respectable in academia. Particularly with the proliferation of free-standing policy and research institutes, over the years more that was relevant has been done.

However, the profound effects of careerism on researchers, the narrow academic focus that is learned at universities, and the habit of taking refuge in slippery assumptions of objectivity—all these distance many social scientists from their human subjects. As if in a painting by Edward Hopper, social scientists gaze off at an angle from their human subjects, alienated from them.

The Politicality of Knowledge

A further reason for the failure of social science to inform policy that I stumbled on is what Hylan Lewis, a sociologist with unassuming honesty, called "the politicality of knowledge." In other words, knowledge and the political climate cannot easily be separated. Here, I discuss research of convenience, on one hand, and research as a patsy, on the other.

Research of Convenience   Each era appears to call for a certain kind of knowledge and to bring it forth. Prior to World War II, when comparatively few women worked, research demonstrated that working mothers tended to have delinquent children. After the war, when many more women were working, social scientists reviewed the earlier research. Then they discerned that children were not led into delinquency because their mothers worked. Only those who received irregular care, whether or not their mothers worked, showed a tendency to be delinquent. Thus, research or, more exactly, analysis of the research, supported what mothers wanted or needed to do.

In the decades since, we have shifted to a labor market and wage levels which *require* that families have two wage earners.

Many mothers *must* work and so are working. Despite serious debate, by 1986 it was possible to say that:

> . . . it is no longer the view of most mental health professionals that a mother of a young child who holds a job outside the home is necessarily doing harm to the child. All the serious research studies agree on this issue. . . .[15]

Conceding a degree of skepticism on my part, I do not contest this research. I only point out that it did not appear (indeed, quite contrary research appeared) until it was wanted.

Similarly, for many years interracial adoption was regarded as risky. Professionals believed that black children adopted by white parents would not readily be integrated into the family. At the same time, legal abortion was denied to poor people (in the early 1960s, more than twice as many children born to poor people were unwanted as compared to children born to the non-poor—42 and 17 percent respectively).[16] Within a few years, however, as legal abortion became widely available and the birth rate declined, a severe shortage of white children available for adoption developed. *Then* professionals came to believe that interracial adoption might be successful, and the practice took hold. Thus, "new knowledge" made it possible for the supply provided by the poor to respond to the demand for adoptive children.

Research as a Patsy As I have noted, undertaking research is itself a political act. Research may be staged mainly to create familiarity with and acceptance of a new idea. The Ford Foundation's so-called "gray area" projects of the early 1960s are an example. Ostensibly, they were to be tests of the effectiveness of community-based social services in opening opportunity in depressed areas. As a result, it was hoped, juvenile delinquency would decline. The War Against Poverty's Community Action Program was conceived along the lines of this "opportunity program" model just as evidence from the "gray area" projects was beginning to come in. Although the picture was cloudy, one would have had to read the evidence, if at all, as casting doubt on the enterprise.[17] Just as a tree that falls in the forest makes no noise, experience that falls on deaf ears teaches nothing. But opportunity programs had been given currency as a practical idea when the government needed one.

These elements of the politicality of knowledge—that research may provide the proof that the moment requires, that it may more exactly be a precursor to than a cause of action, and that it may fail to deal at all with some important questions—are straightforward. More awkward to face is a claim of knowledge (though it may be dubious) or withholding knowledge (that seems sound) for political effect.

A Claim of Knowledge   I draw an example of each from the imbroglio over President Nixon's negative income tax—the Family Assistance Plan (FAP). FAP was complex and embattled and in early 1970 its prognosis was "guarded." In New Jersey, an experiment staged to test whether assuring people a small income might lead them to reduce their work effort had been in the field little more than a year. The researchers were reluctant to make any report. Nevertheless, there was heavy pressure to say something that would reassure Wilbur Mills, chairman of the House Ways and Means Committee, who was concerned about the question of work effort. A *New York Times* Sunday Magazine article describes how Daniel Patrick Moynihan (then head of domestic policy in the White House) "jumped all over" John Wilson, the research director of the Poverty Program. "That's the trouble with you economists," Moynihan said, "you never have any facts until it is too late."[18] Wilson vowed to get some answers.

A report from the New Jersey experiment was shortly provided that left "the impression that the data are quite strong in supporting the Family Assistance Plan (e.g., showing that there is no significant decrease in work effort)."[19] Several months later, upon congressional request, the General Accounting Office produced a sharp critique of the report. The New Jersey experiment had not yet produced enough data upon which to draw conclusions, GAO said, and what there was had not been adequately analyzed.

In the end, the experiment showed that, when guaranteed a small income, there was an apparent decline in work activity among two particular groups: mothers with young children who chose to stay at home and men who took a little longer to shop for the best job they could get. Such results may not seem especially damaging to FAP, though at the time some thought that they were. In any event, they were different from what had been reported under heavy pressure. Meanwhile, however, the earlier report was publicized and the political purpose to revivify FAP had been served.

Withholding Knowledge   At about the same time, the Department of Health, Education and Welfare contracted with National Analysts, a consultant firm in Philadelphia, to study the effectiveness of a welfare incentive formula similar to the one in FAP, which allowed recipients to retain a percentage of increased earnings. The conclusion, inimical to FAP, was that such a provision was not encouraging work because neither recipients nor their workers could understand how the formula operated. HEW withheld the study from publication. After FAP died the report appeared, in four volumes.

It is not only government that may be guilty of manipulation. In Chapter 7, I gave an account of a housing project evaluation that the Community Service Society declined to publish because lay committee members thought it might undermine social work. Does no one count up the number of warm and positive evaluations that appear, of which there is not a trace two years later? Not a few professors content themselves with submitting confidential, scrupulously correct reports when they study public issues for community agencies; but, for one pragmatic reason or another, neither they nor the agencies publish this work.

Institutional Decline: Another Limit of Reason

Bureaucracy—the surrealistic separation of activities from their purposes, the tendency for functions to become more important than people—can contribute heavily to altering or obscuring formal policy. In time, it seems that the policy itself was not sound, even though with a properly functioning organization it might have been. For years, I thought of bureaucracy as a thing in itself, a self-contained, stubborn opponent that could barely be fathomed but had to be tamed.

With more experience, I have come to see the problem more broadly and deeply. I see bureaucracies as living creatures, a product of their histories, environments, staffs and structures.[20] It takes talent and resources to build them sound and user-friendly. Conversely, they may deliberately be built not to function well. Or, a skillful campaign can bring them down; consult, for example, Stuart Butler's unabashed prescription for undermining social security and its bureaucracy.[21] Or, bureaucracies may be subverted by poor management strategies in resonance with adverse external social forces.

As an example of this last, I outline the decline of public child welfare: the system of county and state programs that protect and care for neglected and abused children.

Public Child Welfare   Prior to the 1960s, the ideology of child welfare was clear: a family-centered service, serving all classes, not directed to solving financial problems, using well-trained professionals. (Theory held that financial problems would be dealt with by social security and welfare.) To be sure, the program reached only a minority of the children who needed help, but it operated reasonably well and the leaders of the field had a clear vision of their objectives.

From the 1960s on, child welfare suffered a series of blows that left the program in a shambles. Citizen interest in protecting children diminished. (Women who had earlier been barred from the workplace had invested their energies in this cause, but now they were occupied with regular jobs.) The employment standard to which child welfare workers had previously been held—a graduate degree in social work—was abandoned and a push was on to use paraprofessionals. (There were not enough graduate social workers, anyway.) And at higher administrative levels, professional social workers were replaced by businessmen and women. (The latter would make better managers, or so it was thought. In any event, they often turned out to be less mission-oriented.)

Next, developments such as an increase in single-parent families and more prevalent substance abuse added to child welfare's caseload. Family income among poorer families started a steady decline in 1973 and inflation-adjusted AFDC payment levels declined by almost half in the next twenty years. Thus, changes in family structure and deepening poverty swelled the stream of children who needed protection and foster care.

Another blow to child welfare agencies came in 1962, with the identification of child abuse as a specific family and social problem. The model of child abuse that legislatures and the public bought was a so-called medical model: A distinguishable pathological agent had attacked the abusive family and would disappear if treated in a prescribed manner.[22] None of this characterizes child abuse accurately, but belief in the medical model leads to public frustration with, if not fury at, social workers when child abuse persists. Meanwhile, focusing on child abuse produced thousands of additional children needing attention and care.

In the same period, researchers began to report that children in foster family homes were doing very badly. Many had been moved from one foster home to another, growing more disturbed with each move. These findings "rocked the profession."[23] Then, an influential book advanced the premise that child welfare workers were too indecisive, failing to sever children's ties to wholly uncaring or pathological parents so they could be moved into adoptive homes.[24] In the professional controversy that followed, the interests of parents and children appeared to be in conflict. That is, if only neglectful parents would let go, adoptive parents would be found who would give children what they required. This appearance reinforced an inclination, fostered by public indignation, to remove children from their homes.

Still, the impetus of the critique of foster care began to lead to restraint in placing children and, in 1980, Congress enacted the Adoption Assistance and Child Welfare Act. It was intended both to support keeping a child at home, and to move agencies to take custody more promptly when this seemed best.

Over the years, professional controversy and public attitudes shoved child welfare agencies from a mission of "strengthening families" (that is, maintaining children in their homes) to "child saving" (that is, removing abused children to the safety of foster homes)—and then shoved the agencies back again. A quarter of a million children were in foster care in 1961; the number increased to half a million by 1977. Six years later, the number had dropped to a quarter of a million again, and by 1995 it was once more at half a million.

Although the decade of the 1980s began with the fine words of the Adoption Assistance and Child Welfare Act, federal funding for child welfare was cut by 25 percent. Among other difficulties, this created pressure on child welfare agencies to save money by leaving children in the parental home. Professional leaders taught that deciding when to maintain a child at home and when to arrange foster placement requires delicate judgment, but delicate judgment requires time for exploration and skilled and committed staff; by the 1980s, time was short and such staff were gone or going.

Almost unnoticed, criticism and blame led to increasing routinization of the work of line staff members. Congress began to legislate the content of their work, state legislatures enacted requirements for twenty-four-hour response times and six-month reviews, regulations descended on local agencies in an ungentle snow, and supervisors became more and more pre-scriptive. The line worker's job became routine and simplistic—in a word, stultifying.

Two effects were worker burnout and high turnover. Fifty percent turnover of staff a year became typical. Inevitably, the keenest and most mission-oriented workers tended to depart, leaving behind those who were awaiting retirement or could not find other work. One indicator: During the thirty years between 1958 and 1988, when the proportion of the population with college degrees tripled, the proportion of child welfare workers with college degrees dropped from 62 to 28 percent.[25]

The institution called public child welfare was taking a steady pounding. Because it was perforce serving virtually only poor children and because it was observably doing a poor job, middle-class people would not use the agency (except to adopt a child, for which it was the chief resource, or for residential psychiatric treatment, which was otherwise prohibitively ex-pensive). Thus, having largely lost women's volunteered time, child welfare was stripped of all other outside informed lay criticism and support.

As with a cybernovel, one can enter an analysis of child welfare at any point and go around and around the same characters and the same forces. Public obloquy meant micro-management, and reduced funding as well. In turn, these led to loss of the best staff. Overwork led to poor performance and burnout. Children received poor care. Frequent and abrupt shifts of policy led to confused professional performance. Apart from some embattled administrators, few were inclined to defend the agencies. No solution works because it is over-whelmed by the accumulation of problems, and sullen staffs are uninterested, anyway.

It is an appalling story, even when only sketchily outlined. Each adverse development compounded others and further tangled the tangled skein that requires straightening out. Pa-thology is given body in a bureaucracy that is not so much an

organism designed for a task as an ill-considered, reeling, stu-
porous work in progress. That is, a bureaucracy's staff and the
way they operate in large measure manifest the pressures the
bureaucracy faces, its environment and its history.

Is all or much of this subject to reason? With differences in
specifics, to be sure, most of the major public services—child
welfare, welfare, education—suffer from the same general
problems. Misguided employment policies, income maintenance and tax policies, and policies that determine residential
patterns, not to mention changing demography and economies,
sap their capacity to perform their functions. These combine
with underfunding, poor staffing and public resentment.
Adapting to these changes and problems distorts bureaucracies
in a manner that further undermines pursuit of their ostensible
mission. Bureaucracy as a four-letter word is not a function of
age; it is a function of subversion, deliberate or unconscious.

Such bureaucracies as the one characterized here effectively operate without policy. Research and analysis, in particular the kinds that focus narrowly on whether "top-down
administration" works better than "bottom-up administration"
or specialized caseloads work better than so-called generic
caseloads, do not address the central problem. Nor, on the
evidence, does reason affect the complex of problems described
here, which arises from our culture, our values and our political
process. Has anyone claimed that these are subject to reason?

Do Research and Advocacy Seriously Affect Policy?
Well, no, and on occasion, yes. Two studies, separated by thirty
years, frame my view about how much independent influence
policy work may have.

In France in 1963, studying social security and social services, I gave special attention to a unique French institution, the
family union. Family unions were financed by the government
to provide family-oriented social services and to lobby the
government in support of family interests.

To the distress of leaders of the family unions and, no doubt, churlishly repaying the openness and hospitality they had accorded to me, I had to conclude that they were relatively ineffective. They had seemed effective, indeed powerful, when, after World War II, the country wanted what they wanted: larger families, enriched family allowances, family housing. Fifteen years later, the country had lost interest in these objectives and the family unions lost power. "We see the family unions more as instruments of national policy than as movers of policy," I wrote.[26]

I have indicated that, a few years later, I was a consultant to The [British] Committee on Local Authority and Allied Personal Social Services—the Seebohm Committee, as it was known. In time, it presented the government with an ambitious set of recommendations which were duly implemented. The centralized local social service departments (SSDs) which a reorganization established appeared to work well—in terms of service, in terms of professionalism and in terms of financing. Serious difficulties developed over the years, however, and, in 1991, the Joseph Rowntree Foundation invited me to spend a year evaluating the functioning and situation of the SSDs.

I was naturally intrigued with the question whether we had planned well. Might we have foreseen the difficulties and planned better? It seemed not.

> . . . the policies that were prescribed for the social service departments [I wrote] reflected the climate and the needs of the 1960s and, arguably, the early 1970s. There may have been vision but it did not encompass a sweeping change in government, social pessimism, economic downturn in the 1970s and late 1980s and family change, nor could it reasonably be expected to do so.[27]

Separated by time and perspective though they were, the

French and British studies suggest complementary points. As in the British experience, our views and convictions are more a product of the social and political climate that envelops us than we have any idea. (Named by arrangement with a Labor government, the Seebohm Committee's recommendations were implemented by a Conservative government. Both British governments were enveloped by the same climate.) Like the French family unions, all institutions (and all scholarly disciplines) are creatures of society. Though some may feel themselves adversarial, with few exceptions they are doing society's work on society's terms.

Then, do research and advocacy seriously affect policy? Not in large ways, generally. In small ways, yes, if they assimilate and embrace the social and political climate. Still, the climate is always changing. Sensing that this is happening or is possible is what draws reformers on.

How, Then, Does Policy Move?

We get movement in social policy out of the resonance of developments that are quite unrelated to social science and may be unrelated to reason. For example, the Poverty Program and the Elementary and Secondary Education Act came in a time and manner dictated by more powerful developments than the long-standing need for reform: the guilt of a decade of dividing affluence among the affluent; the death of John F. Kennedy and the inauguration of Lyndon Baines Johnson, with all the passion and ambition that were aroused; and the turning in frustration of the still powerful civil rights movement to goals it *could* achieve. Further, the desperate plight of older cities—most of them with Democratic mayors at a time when the president was also a Democrat—dictated a program designed so federal money would circumvent states and go directly to cities.

Social scientists play a role but most often a role shaped by an "invisible hand." This is the message of much that this chapter says. They may be wholly unaware of being influenced by their institution or the general climate of opinion, just as we earthlings are unaware of being swept around the sun at twenty miles a second.

On the other hand, social scientists coalesce around assumptions and conclusions—financial incentives, the effect of maternal deprivation, culture of poverty—that leak into public conversation and in time *become* the climate. It is not entirely important whether these assumptions and concepts originate with social scientists or derive from public bias in the first place. In that case, they legitimate and support the public bias. As with the French family unions, often these ideas are conservative.[28] This is not surprising; professionals may have much to conserve.

I should somewhat exempt from these observations what another prominent (and controversial) sociologist, James Coleman, called "procedural questions": Do children learn better in small classes, or not? Does parent education educate parents? Are food stamps used to buy food or are they sold for money to pay the rent or buy drugs? The detailed answers arising from such work often alter practice.[29]

What Was This to Me?

In laying out what appear to me to be limits of reason, I describe difficulties about which I had to learn and with which I had to grapple. Social science was my natural teacher and ally. Dealing with it was like growing up—I had to qualify my respect for it with a persistent skepticism about its conventional or dogmatic assertions. I had to seek its support—for its support would be vital for an advocate like me—without romanticizing it or exaggerating its validity. In this search for balance and my own judgment of what was real, a considerable help was marginality, which I have now mentioned several times.

A capacity to maintain my distance and a penchant for unpopular conclusions were useful in another sense. I faced the need to reconcile my consciousness of being partisan with a certain fastidiousness about the conduct of intellectual inquiry. One must necessarily be scrupulous if each separate omission or defect, whether significant or not, is likely to be held to contaminate the substance of an argument.

In my view, the hope for policy studies, at least in terms of the engagement of social science, lies in the ideals of integrity and scientific rigor that are taught in class and may be modeled by leaders of the field. Ideologies may be passed on even when they are not practiced, to come alive when the times permit or demand. In the midst of the "but-everyone-does-it" moral corruption that is widely evidenced these days, and even at the cost of government and foundation grants and unpopularity, social scientists may hold to such ideals and discover their considerable satisfactions.

As did Lynd and Becker, I think it fitting as well that social scientists give special sympathy to the problems and views of the underprivileged. It would make a suitable corrective. By the nature of their class and status, social scientists are suffused in the views and interests of the privileged; there is no danger that these views will fail to be represented in their work. With such an attitude and with compassion we may help to win the world, or it may not be won.

NOTES

1. Alvin L. Schorr, "Beyond Pluck and Luck," *Journal of Home Economics,* 54, no. 4, April 1962.

2. E. Franklin Frazier, *Black Bourgeoisie: The Rise of a New Middle Class in the United States,* Free Press, Glencoe, Illinois, 1957.

3. Alfred Kazin, "The Past Breaks Out," quoted in William Zinsser, *Inventing the Truth: The Art and Craft of Memoir,* Houghton Mifflin Co., Boston, 1987, p. 95.

4. Heather I. Ross and Isabel V. Sawhill, *Time of Transition,* The Urban Institute, Washington, D.C., 1975.

5. For a contrary example when attention was paid, see Katherine S. Newman, "What Inner-City Jobs for Welfare Moms?" *New York Times,* 20 May 1995.

6. Nigel S. Paneth, "The Problem of Low Birth Weight," *The Future of Children*, 5, no. 1, Spring 1995.

7. Erving Goffman, "The Interaction Order," Presidential Address to the American Sociological Association, *American Sociological Review*, 48, February 1982, pp. 1-17.

8. United Nations, Consultative Group on the Prevention of Crime and Treatment of Offenders, "The Economics of Training in Social Defense," working paper prepared by the Secretariat, 8 July 1968, and draft report prepared by P. J. Woodfield, 13 August 1968, Geneva.

9. Ford Foundation Project on Social Welfare and the American Future, *The Common Good—Social Welfare and the American Future*, New York, May 1989, p. 13.

10. For indications of possible damage to children, see Alvin L. Schorr, "Welfare in Actual Life," (Cleveland) *Plain Dealer*, 21 December 1994. See also Ellen Galinsky, *The Study of Children in Family Child Care and Relative Care*, Families and Work Institute, New York, 1994. Very late, to be sure, MDRC did in the end begin to focus on the children. For example, see Dan Bloom, *After AFDC: Welfare-to-Work Choices and Challenges for the States*, Manpower Demonstration Research Corporation, New York, 1997.

11. Robert S. Lynd, *Knowledge for What?*, Princeton University Press, New Haven, Connecticut, 1939, p. 2.

12. Howard Becker, "Whose Side Are We On?" Presidential Address to the Society for the Study of Social Problems, *Social Problems*, 14, 1967, pp. 230–47.

13. Task Force on Social Work Research, *Building Social Work Knowledge for Effective Services and Policies: A Plan for Research Development*, Austin, Texas, 1991, pp. v, 16.

14. Stanley L. Witkin, "Whither Social Work Research: An Essay Review," *Social Work*, 40, no. 3, May 1995, p. 425.

15. Stella Chess,"Woman's Work," *Readings*, 1, no. 1, March 1986, p. 23.

16. Charlotte Muller, "Socioeconomic Outcomes of Present Abortion Policy," paper prepared for Workshop on Abortion, Bethesda, Maryland, 15–16 December 1969.

17. Peter Marris and Martin Rein, *Dilemmas of Reform: Poverty and Community Action in the United States*, Atherton Press, New York, 1967.

18. Fred J. Cook, "When You Just Give Money to the Poor," *New York Times Magazine*, 3 May 1970, p. 110.

19. Walter Williams, *The Struggle for a Negative Income Tax*, Chapter IV, "The Experiment and the Family Assistance Plan," Institute of Governmental Research, University of Washington, Seattle, 1972.

20. Like many discoveries, this had been detected by others earlier. See Anthony Downs, *Inside Bureaucracy*, Chapter 2, "The Life Cycle of Bureaus," HarperCollins, New York, 1967. See also Richard J. Stillman II, *The American Bureaucracy*, Chapter 3, "External Forces Shaping Modern Bureaucracy," Nelson Hall, Chicago, 1987.

21. Stuart M. Butler, "For Serious Action on Privatization," *Journal of the Institute for Socioeconomic Studies*, X, no. 2, Summer 1985.

22. Barbara Nelson, *Making an Issue of Child Abuse*, University of Chicago Press, Chicago, 1984.

23. Susan Whitelaw Downs, ed., *Foster Care Reform in the '70s: Final Report of the Permanency Planning Dissemination Project*, School of Social Work, Portland State University, Portland, Oregon, 1981.

24. J. Goldstein, Anna Freud, and Albert Solnit, *Beyond the Best Interests of the Child*, Free Press, Glencoe, Illinois, 1973.

25. Report of the Advisory Council on CWS, Children's Bureau, U.S. Department of Health, Education and Welfare, Washington, D.C., 28 December 1959. Mimeographed. Also, U.S. General Accounting Office, "Foster Care —Incomplete Implementation of the Reforms and Unknown Effectiveness," Washington, D.C., August 1989. 1958 and 1988 are offered for this comparison because surveys happen to have been done and reported for those years. Note: In 1958, according to the Advisory Council report above, 28 percent of caseworkers in child welfare had at least two years of graduate training in social work.

26. Alvin L. Schorr, *Social Security and Social Services in France*, Research Report no. 7, Social Security Administration, U.S. Government Printing Office, Washington, D.C., 1965, p. 19.

27. Alvin L. Schorr, *The Personal Social Services: An Outside View*, Joseph Rowntree Foundation, York, U.K., July 1992, p. 6.

28. See Sanford F. Schram, *Words of Welfare: The Poverty of Social Science and the Social Science of Poverty*, University of Minnesota Press, Minneapolis, 1996. Schram argues that social research is conducted in a manner that will support public policy and tends to deepen stigma for those who are already stigmatized.

29. James S. Coleman, "Conflicts Between Policy Research and Policy Making," paper prepared for Conference on Israeli Education, Van Leer Foundation, Jerusalem, August 1977. Typescript.

Punctuated Equilibrium

I have always written in the midst of social tension and the flux of policy—rarely more so than now. The policies and politics I was trying to order and improve were changing as I worked, and the tide of reaction that I perceived twenty or twenty-five years ago has now, in 1996, crashed through the institutional structure of the welfare state.

As this book has been several years in the writing, a chapter at a time taken up and completed, Chapter 4 about welfare was completed before it seemed at all conceivable that the federal AFDC program would be quite wiped out, as it has now been. Not more than three years elapsed between that chapter and this one, but this is a sign of how fast matters moved. By 1996, we were prepared to abandon all vestiges of community and transform ourselves into a winner-take-all and, more gravely, a loser-lose-all society.

In a conversation with John Gardner in 1966, when he was secretary of HEW, I confessed to always having thought that, with backslides and missteps, to be sure, ever so slowly our society improves. After all, we learn a little more every year, and as we become richer we can afford to be more humanitarian. By 1966, however, it seemed that change did not occur like that at all. Rather, social conditions stagnate, without much improvement, producing pressing needs and ideas good and bad, until the intersection of powerful events (in that case, unprecedented affluence, the civil rights movement, the Kennedy assassination, the Johnson presidency) opens a window for reform. The reforms we were contemplating, all enacted in a

two-year period, included the Civil Rights Act of 1964, the
Elementary and Secondary Education Act, the Poverty Program, the Food Stamp Act, Medicare and Medicaid.

The lesson we took was that one must always be ready,
because opportunities for implementing good ideas would not
come often and then the window might abruptly slam shut.
One notes that this was all about reform; there was nothing
about reaction. However carefully I had studied to be tough
and calculating, I retained a romantic streak.

Drawing an analogy from evolutionary biology, today I
replace the window-of-opportunity theory with a theory of
punctuated equilibrium: There is a stately tide of social progress or regress—I have seen the tide come and seen it go and it
is there!—which is interrupted from time to time by a florid
eruption of radical ideas and policies.* The mid-1930s, the
mid-1960s and the mid-1990s were good years for eruptions,
whatever a numerologist may make of that.

Many of the new ideas are freakish and do not survive
even long enough to be assigned a family or a phylum. Others
may change the policy landscape forever, for good or ill. They
may have been carefully prepared, or may be propelled by little
more than a macho thrust to wipe out the old (*"It is broke"*) and
bring in the new.

As with evolutionary biology, mine is far from an "onward
and upward" theory and there is little in it to celebrate. We may
think that humankind was the goal towards which all biological
evolution pointed and we may think that the "welfare state" or
the "democratic, free-market state" was the goal towards which
all social evolution pointed, but this is because it is we who
stand at this self-anointed pinnacle. Different resolutions of
long-ago contests and catastrophes, wholly unrelated to the

---

*The biological theory of "punctuated equilibrium" holds that stasis in evolution
"should be an expected norm . . ., and that evolution should be concentrated in brief
episodes of branching speciation." Stephen Jay Gould, Dinosaur in a Haystack,
Harmony Books, 1995, p. 127.

principles and dogmas we deal with today, might have led to quite other outcomes—which would also be regarded by the current victors as pinnacles. Anticipating such a view, Henry Adams dismissed "the fiction that society . . . aimed at a conscious purpose."[1]

Then How Does One Take a Stand?

If a person is to be a factor at all in the erratic course of social evolution—and with talent, luck and an offshore tide, a few people turn out to be considerable factors—a stand has to be based, first of all, on one's deepest convictions. Mine are displayed throughout these pages: egalitarianism, sympathy and respect for the underdog, a sense of community (experienced as a youth) and a belief in the need to foster it; a view that government is a creature of the people and owes them empathy and responsiveness.

The chief adversary of such convictions is the profound greed that has seized the nation; it has been coming on for decades. I recall that a 1975 report on philanthropy prompted me to do an extended essay on "a new greed" in the *Washington Post*.[2] After a two-year study, the national Commission on Private Philanthropy and Public Needs had proposed income tax deductions of 150 to 200 percent! for charitable contributions. The sweetened deduction might increase charitable gifts by $9.8 billion, of which $7.4 billion would be revenue forgone by the government. Thus, the government would foster philanthropy by buying it—$3 for $1, an irony hardly to be borne. However, we were already so far gone in judging everything by money that the irony escaped notice. Ronald Reagan assumed the presidency a few years later and, in his charming way, legitimized greed for any who might have felt a trace of doubt.

It has been my view that, just as our values create our institutions, in turn our institutions and social structures *create* our values. Thus, social security *created* the modern concept of retirement[3] and French children's allowances undergird the devotion of the French to children. Even apart from believing that if we created the institutions the values would follow, I rarely wrote about values per se because it seemed hard to do without sounding pious or vague. However, the pervasive greed that has settled upon Americans is a thing in itself now, making it almost irrelevant to argue for truly community-centered policies. So I place first in this matter of taking a stand the examination and assertion of one's deepest principles and an attempt to take back the public debate from our grossest social predators and their attendant rationalizers and flacks.

However, economic and institutional developments constrain whether we can find our way back to a decent society. I turn to some of these.

Economic Developments

It is well and widely understood that we live and work in an economy considerably changed from two or three decades ago. Fundamental economic changes have been accompanied by sharp losses in the share of national income by middle-income and poorer people. Other changes—poorer education, more widespread single parenthood, the dramatic increase of women in the labor force and shrinking government transfers—have certainly contributed to a loss of share at lower incomes.

This loss of share reflects, in part, a long, slow fall in the median wage for those without a college education—who are most of the workforce. Every year, more families with a full-time working member are poor. Moonlighting is a growing phenomenon: By 1994, seven million Americans held multiple jobs, almost half of them—a new development—women.

The chief economic changes are generally identified as: 1) the development of a global economy, which allows corporations to shift production from one country to another to gain market or wage advantage or to lower taxes; 2) rapid technological development, simultaneously demanding wholly unskilled workers (who can be paid very little) and workers with higher skills (which many who want jobs cannot acquire); and 3) a financial and management "culture" which equates efficient management with laying off workers. As to this last, it is widely remarked with amazement, though financiers are not amazed, that stock market indexes are automatically puffed up by layoffs.

People who write about and discuss such matters—whom the British call "the chattering classes"—have not seemed disposed to criticize this employer culture but there *has* been criticism, notably in a recent book by David Gordon.

Gordon argues that the embrace by American management of what he calls "the stick strategy"—threats, pressures, layoffs—rather than an incentive strategy has required more bureaucracy for enforcement. Thus, while all ranks of workers have suffered dismissals, the lowest paid have suffered most; and the proportion of supervisors to line workers has gone up. This change that he notes is a fact. Holding down pay levels for line workers to pay for more supervisors to keep them in line, Gordon writes, is one reason for the increasingly unequal distribution of income.[4]

Other economic developments antedate the globalization, technological development and tough management culture which have matured in the last years, and are reinforced by them. In particular, in the last thirty years, we have gone over from an expectation and, in large measure, a practice of full-time work with extended tenure to work that is part-time and temporary. With the decline of labor union membership, the latter occupations, never strongly unionized anyway, suffer particularly acutely in pay and benefits. Even workers who were permanent, in principle, are now understood to be subject to termination at any time.

Thus, 30 percent of the workforce is now "contingent" labor—contract workers, consultants, the self-employed, part-timers and temporary workers.[5] Some workers, particularly those who have retirement incomes or who have reason to want to work at home, are pleased with contingent status. On the other hand, many do not earn nearly enough—and they suffer as well from one of the very reasons that industry prefers contingent workers: They do not get health or pension benefits.

From 1979 to 1995, more than forty-three million jobs were lost in the United States. Each federal administration explains that new jobs were created simultaneously, but one out of four of the people who lost jobs is still unemployed a year later. Only a third of those who do find work earn as much as they did before being laid off.[6] When experienced at close hand, numbers like these take on a grim reality. Nearly three-quarters of all households in the country, the *New York Times* reported in 1996, had a "close encounter with layoffs since 1980."[7] That is, a family member, a relative, a friend or a neighbor was laid off.

All this is outlined to make three general points. First, it is not tolerable that our labor market should be driven by wage competition with underdeveloped countries. For many years, we paid higher wages than even employers in European countries and competed with them successfully because we were more inventive and productive and had a better trained workforce and better management. The notion that we are now reduced to trading the life style of our working people for foreign trade and corporate profit is a paradigm shift in thinking.

Wholly free markets of the sort that are being sold to us are *not* typical of thriving Asian nations or the European Community. The latter mixes managed and free markets and all its member countries spend far more than we do in the public sector. Such a course for the United States, mixing a free market with countervailing public institutions and processes, is laid out by economist Robert Kuttner, for one, who writes:

> In a nutshell, my thesis is that America's devotion to *laissez-faire* as an ideal for either the U.S. economy or

world commerce has become a serious hazard. It impedes the tasks of defining our strategic goals in the world, restoring our own economy to health, and organizing a sustainable, plural new economic order.[8]

Second, the trends that have been outlined present the serious risk that as a large portion of American industry goes multinational, it will quite escape national control. In such a circumstance, there can be no domestic social policy. We shall return to this.

Third, these trends have consequences for our spirit as well as for the American standard of living. The anxiety and depression of millions of workers who are unemployed or who fear that they may be dismissed at any time contribute to an epidemic mood that requires attention. This problem deserves a caption of its own.

"Things Fall Apart; the Centre Cannot Hold. . . ."[9]
It is not new to complain about the rapidity of change. In 1611, three hundred years before the composition of Yeats' famous poem, John Donne complained about the effect of scientific developments on the sense of a stable world:

> And new philosophy calls all in doubt,
> The Element of fire is quite put out;
> The Sun is lost and th'earth, and no man's wit
> Can well direct him where to look for it.
>
> . . . 'Tis all in pieces, all coherence gone;
> All just supply, and all Relation:
> Prince, Subject, Father, Sonne, are things forgot.[10]

Poets are the canaries of society; they sniff oncoming doom.

Much later, just a hundred years ago, Emile Durkheim, a pioneer sociologist, discovered that certain types of suicide are a consequence of too rapid social change.[11] Whether change means an improvement or decline in one's circumstances is not critical in this matter; positive and negative change both upset people, and suicides increase.

If not a new phenomenon, today social change moves at an unsurpassed pace. Economic changes, as well as changes induced or permitted by technology (in communication, in socializing), in family patterns and patterns of sexual behavior, in continuous subjection to information, entertainment and advertising, in patterns of work, in gender relations, in ethnic relationships, in the widespread use of mood-altering drugs and in the fact or perception of increasing crime—all produce a sense of chaos.

Compounding the impact of the pace and magnitude of change, the authority of the church and other institutions to which people looked for stability for centuries has, in this century, been undermined by the general advance of relativism —in the laws of physics (the theory of relativity), in the meaning of language (postmodern deconstructionism), in the very laws of human psychology (psychoanalysis).

This is George Steiner's thesis: People's lives were once given structure by the moral authority they accepted, which has now been eroded by the view that ideas and faith do not have intrinsic validity. Beliefs are perishable products of our time and culture. Steiner attributes to the consequent decline of institutional authority a primitive thirst for authority and a desperate acceptance of simple dogmas such as religious and civic fundamentalism (for example, religious cults and citizen militias).[12] Many who do not turn to such flaky supports are left feeling entirely lost.

One must add to the anxiety about rapid and, apparently, accelerating change—unopposed by deep faith or trust—other simultaneously developing sources of strain. For one, the functioning of American families is considerably altered in a manner (many more single-parent families; the norm that, in a two-parent family, both parents work) that places considerable strain on every member of the family. Much has been written about this and it is not necessary to add to that literature here. Not as widely understood are the strains produced by unemployment and "relative deprivation."

Unemployment and Anxiety About Being Unemployed

Unemployment and anxiety about unemployment have far-reaching consequences. Marie Jahoda, a prominent psychologist, has identified five elements of rootedness or discipline that are disturbed or destroyed by unemployment. They are "the experience [or structuring] of time, the reduction of social contacts, the lack of participation in collective purposes, the absence of an acceptable status and its consequences for personal identity, and the absence of regular activity."[13] (This is a dense black hole of a quotation; a slow rereading may be justifiable.)

In all these ways, the unemployed are led to feel disorganized and deprived. One need not wonder at the fact that the single most disabling quality in terms of capacity to work is extended unemployment. Psychological effects like despair, depression and child abuse were widely reported during the recession of the 1980s. In a study for Congress, M. Harvey Brenner established a connection between the unemployment rate and, six years later, increased rates of suicide, homicide and mental hospital admissions. He cited like findings in European countries.[14] In 1996, other American scholars repeated the analysis and came to a similar conclusion.[15]

Relative Deprivation and Unfair Shares

Economic conditions and psychological and physical health interact in ways that are obvious but also in ways that may be obscure. A classic British study lays out two conditions that lead to a sense of "relative deprivation" or grievance. One is a person's position relative to others: How removed in status does he perceive himself from others with whom he compares himself? Second is a person's state of expectation: How does she judge her chances or likelihood of self-improvement?[16]

A large gap between one's relative position and expectations tends to magnify a sense of grievance; a small gap or low expectations tend to diminish it. In American ideology, of course, everyone can get ahead. This belief leads to the most ambitious and hopeful expectations and so—with the positions of Americans nevertheless very disparate—the sense of grievance balloons. Thirty years ago, the National Commission on the Causes and Prevention of Violence thought this tension between high expectations and low relative achievement a primary reason for our high crime rate.[17]

Yet the inequality has grown much worse. One hears the grievance framed, for example, in the complaint that children once did better than their parents; now children cannot even expect to do as well. The trend may be summed up with a rule-of-thumb ratio that technicians use to measure inequality. The ratio reflects the relationship between the total income of the poorest and the richest fifths of the population.

For as long as the Census had measured it, this ratio was 8 to 1. The richest fifth of the population had eight times as much total income as the poorest fifth. In the last two decades, the ratio has climbed steadily to 9 to 1 in 1982, to 10 to 1 in 1986 and to 11 to 1 in 1994.[18] It is a shocking disproportion—more extreme than anything we have recorded and more extreme than in almost any comparable country.[19] Among effects other than fueling crime and the population's sense of grievance, a careful and unimpeached stream of research leads to the conclusion that the rate of physical and mental illness in an industrial society is related to its level of inequality. ". . . [W]hen socio-economic differences are narrowed, population health status improves."[20]

In short, our citizens struggle, with the greatest difficulty, to adjust to an accelerating rate of change. Adding to this, we are eroding the living standards of the less-than-rich population, depriving many of their jobs or the confidence that their jobs are secure and building a sense of grievance about a severe, steady and real loss of share in the economy. These burdens and anxieties are profound and widespread; we add them to others with which families must deal. The strains have so far broken out in the dysfunction and hostility, in the resignation and alienation, in the coldness and meanness that are seen everywhere.

The Barbell Phenomenon

A barbell is a bar with adjustable weights (bells) at each end; as one pulls one bell closer the other bell retreats. In this figure of speech, let one end of the barbell represent major social issues, which we now review.

Parallel with recent changes in the distribution of income, debate about public policy has shifted from the premise that the government should not intrude into the behavior of citizens to "a deepening concern for the development of character in the citizenry" and "a growing awareness that a variety of public problems can only be understood . . . if they are seen as arising out of a defect in character formation."[21] The country has shifted from a nonjudgmental approach to public policy to "the notion that public life should express the moral convictions and shape the moral character of citizens."[22] One notes that this is a formulation for social engineering, if ever there was one.

There may be no better example of this shift than the fate of an arcane requirement in the social security law that AFDC benefits should be provided as an "unrestricted cash payment." Anyone eligible was to receive cash, without restriction of any sort on its use. This provision was seen as a way to maintain or build the self-esteem of recipients and their capacity to exercise independent judgment. Under the pressure of unremitting complaints about the fecklessness of welfare mothers, however, in 1962 Congress authorized "protective payments"—that is, payments to a third party who would spend the money on behalf of selected recipients.

In the following years, the "unrestricted" cash payment was restricted in other ways—by the establishment of the food stamp program (which waxed while AFDC payments waned), by deducting rent money from recipients' checks and paying it directly to landlords (creating new difficulties in getting a dry faucet or a cold radiator repaired) and by reducing the payment if recipients failed to identify the father of their child, to work for a high school equivalency degree, or whatever. By 1990, little remained over which welfare mothers had control. So much for self-esteem and independent judgment!

In the 1960s, such restrictions were justified as ways to teach and to help mothers and their children; by the 1980s, all pretense gone, the determination to coerce specified behavior in mothers was plain. (Children had faded from the conversation.) In 1996, AFDC was put to a protracted death; the very poor who were unable to find work might be left with food stamps, school lunches, public housing or housing vouchers and Medicaid; all useful, but not cash. There would be no cash at all.

Thus, in one strand of its policies, we see welfare's evolution from a practice stubbornly neutral about how people would live to a ferocious effort to shape their behavior. As has often been the case, developments in welfare foreshadowed what was to be a wider social struggle.[23]

Recent decades have seen an impassioned debate about moral rectitude—what Michael Sandel calls "the recrudescence of virtue,"[24] fueled by the very sense of chaos in family and institutional arrangements that is referred to above and by the broad conviction that sexual license, irreligion and crime have risen to new heights (or plunged to new depths). No doubt, national political leaders—unable, after 1985 or so, to think of real solutions to national problems or, given the budget straitjacket in which the country was bound up, unable to propose the expenditures that solutions would require—found it convenient to hold forth on morality, and so contributed to the sense of a fall from virtue.

It would take an essay all its own to disentangle the notions that are conflated in the alarmist view of American moral behavior. For example, it is simply not true that the rate of teenage pregnancy (*"children having children"*) is now higher than it has been in recent decades; in the 1950s, the rate was higher, in fact. (It *is* true, and perhaps this is what people are thinking about, that the proportion of teenage mothers who are unmarried has risen steadily. However, this proportion has increased for *every* age group.[25] Profound changes have taken place in how *women of all ages and all marital statuses* view marriage—because of a woman's capacity these days to support herself and her child without a husband, albeit with difficulty; because of the spread among women of that old-time self-esteem; and because of the consequent fading away of the stigma connected with single parenthood. A characterization of these real-life changes as moral breakdown is obviously arguable.)

Nor is it true by any measure of church membership or attendance or what people say about their beliefs that the country has grown less religious.[26] Nor is it true that the overall crime rate is rising; it has been falling for some time now across the country. In general, much of the scene that is painted to advance a behaviorally oriented public policy is greatly oversimplified or simply incorrect.

If incorrect observations failed to move public policy, we would be a great deal better off than we are. In fact, the new, more judgmental approach has produced a wide range of symbolic, practical and punitive measures—from the removal of offending books from libraries and schools, finding a constitutionally acceptable variant of a prayer for public schools and placing religious symbols in public squares all the way to "three strikes and you're out" prison sentences.

Abortion has become harder to arrange. Between restrictions on the use of federal funds for abortion and the activities of anti-abortion militants, most counties in the United States (84 percent) now have no known professional who will perform an abortion.[27] Contraception, too, has become harder to afford, public funding for this purpose having dropped from $350 million in 1980 to a little more than $250 million (in 1980 dollars) in 1992.[28] And a bill to end no-fault divorce was introduced in the Florida legislature in 1996 and similar campaigns were under way in twenty other states.

Between 1990 and 1994, one-third of our larger American cities adopted curfews for youths for the first time.[29] Most states have changed their laws to make it easier to prosecute juveniles in adult criminal courts, and many have enacted "parental responsibility" laws to allow courts to punish the parents if their child breaks a law.

In the 1980s and 1990s, we spent a good deal of money on the physical embodiment of formal social controls: prisons, community corrections and mental health institutions.[30] Since 1973, the total number of prisoners has multiplied more than four times. Almost 3 percent of men aged fourteen to thirty-four are in jail. And now we have the relatively new phenomenon of "innocent bystander" orphaning of children—an effect of the convergence of rising criminal convictions of mothers (perhaps seventy thousand in 1994) and courts that require that women receive the same sentences as men.[31]

In all these ways, we count the buildup of a didactic public policy insistent on "improving" personal behavior.

The other bell on this barbell might be called "Is Corporate Profit All?" As personal freedom retreats, corporate freedom advances. It may not be entirely strange that public efforts to coerce individuals should accompany increasing freedom for corporations and businesses. As citizens feel shoved about, disregarded, exposed and vulnerable, they turn on one another and especially on the stigmatized families and individuals who have been nominated for such attention by intellectuals[32] and the media. They are not able to turn on corporations, which are heavily defended by conservative ideology and tendentious economics—not to say, by accumulated wealth—and which are increasingly beyond the reach of ordinary citizens.

This is now being dramatized across the country by the transformation of the delivery of medical care in a manner that is extraordinarily upsetting to all except the well-to-do (denial of recommended care, denial of a patient's right to select her physician, etc.). Even physicians—towering in defense of their independent judgment until a few years ago—have by and large yielded passively to control of their medical decisions by burgeoning health care corporations. Then how might a mere patient exercise free choice?

Developments in the health care industry coincide with, and must in part be attributed to, a broad shift from government regulation to deregulation. Otherwise, such anti-competitive practices, so inimical to consumers, would not be permitted for very long.

In the 1970s, regulations concerned with the relation of one business to others that had the effect of limiting competition suffered an onslaught from businesses that felt locked out and from consumers.[33] So, in the last two decades, we have had deregulation of railroads, airlines, natural gas, federal banks, savings and loan associations, cable television and telephone companies. Eventually, environmental or consumer regulations enacted in the 1970s retreated as well: Controls on pollution were relaxed, logging companies were permitted to clear-cut in national forests and the food industry was accorded a measure of self-regulation.

The substantial movement toward deregulation did suffer small eddies and retreats. Cable companies, charged with "arrogance and self-dealing," were subject to *re*regulation in 1992.[34] Angered by Health Maintenance Organization "gag rules," in 1996, sixteen states passed laws to prevent HMOs from limiting what doctors could tell patients.[35] And on hard-fought fronts like gender equality and homosexuals' rights, there were gains as well as losses.

In the 1990s, the movement toward deregulation was swelled by devolution fever—moves to devolve policy judgments and oversight from the federal government to the states. As is recognized everywhere except in political speeches, states find it even harder than the federal government to resist powerful interests. Still, in the 1990s, they were asked to run their own welfare systems and to decide about such matters as highway speed limits, health programs and drinking water standards.

All in all, over the last two decades there has been a considerable net loss for personal freedom and net gain for corporate freedom, the latter—does this need to be said?—in the interests of corporate profit.

One notes that the influence of corporations on public policies grows in tandem with their size and power. As they gather more resources, they are able to invest more heavily in lobbying for even wider deregulation. Indeed, a time comes, as it has already come with large health care corporations, when regulatory agencies find it difficult to discipline them because the penalties would injure so many whom they serve.

If matters go on in this way, there will be no national social policy because, as a byproduct of their conduct of business, whether unwittingly or recklessly, industries will soon dominate social policy.

Flipping the Barbell

It will be terribly difficult to flip the barbell. The broad attempt to coerce the way other people live arises from anxieties that have deep roots, as we have seen. Attempts to coerce behavior are likely seriously to diminish only as the pressures that produce such anxieties are somewhat relieved. As for regulation of businesses, American *laissez-faire* ideology supports *de*regulation. If citizens nevertheless try to regain control, industry is now more than ever in a position to do business outside the United States, that is, outside national constraints.

Still, egregious offenses against the public appear to be generating a backlash; and unfolding developments in health care, with the outrage and dramatic human stories they produce, may well be a flash point in a move back to regulation. Therefore, professionals have begun to review the legal and philosophical basis for more extensive regulation of corporations.

The kind of corporation we have today, with extensive powers and limited liability is a late nineteenth-century invention.[36] Earlier, corporate charters were issued only to serve specific public purposes: to operate a turnpike, a banking system, a canal. Corporations were prohibited from owning other businesses and their property and capital were routinely limited. The government kept the power to alter or revoke charters.[37] By the end of the nineteenth century, however, American corporations had secured acceptance of the legal fiction that they were persons, with broad powers to conduct business.[38]

It is plain, as one reviews the history, that expansion of corporate powers occurred in a context of overriding public purpose—the government's desire to open the frontier and encourage commercial development—and of politically powerful entrepreneurs. On the other hand, it is also plain that, as anxiety about monopoly power or the potential for public harm flared, regulation of corporations increased.

If it is true that a backlash is building, we may be coming into a time when it will be important to think more broadly and deeply about regulation than we are inclined to do. For example, it is trigger-happy and blinkered to legislate, as Congress did in 1996, that a woman having a baby may stay in the hospital at least two days, when no thought is given to medical care for women and children before and after birth and attention to other like limitations of the health care system is studiously avoided.

Recent proposals for a new view of regulation include: re-chartering corporations for limited periods of time, subject to precise restrictions; stripping corporations of "personhood"; prohibiting corporations from making *any* contributions to electoral campaigns; prohibiting corporations from owning other corporations;[39] and giving employees a voice in decisions affecting the viability of their companies.[40] U.S. Senator Jeff Bingaman of New Mexico has proposed formation of a new category of business corporation, the R-Corp (R for "Responsible"), which would receive tax and regulatory benefits in exchange for meeting specified standards of social responsibility.[41]

Such ideas aim at returning corporations more nearly to serving as vehicles of public purpose, to limiting their power and to providing defined participation to those whose lives the corporations most affect. And if we can find the instruments for social control of business, perhaps it will be less necessary to instruct and control our neighbors or, more exactly, the neighbors outside our gates.

To Punctuate the Equilibrium

Citizens have to judge for themselves what the people who have for a little while been in charge—in government and out—intend for the country. Do they care about us nearly as much as they care about themselves? The account above—lower wages, a safety net in tatters, fraying personal freedom, job insecurity, alienation, a steady loss of share in the economy for most of the nation, coldness and meanness everywhere and (one never knows) a brewing eruption of some sort—suggests that they do not. Indeed, they have candidly spread it around that the purest selfishness will produce the best result for all. Well, the result is out there to see.

On the other hand liberals, that is the people who profess to care about us, offer useful, though discrete, program ideas such as are discussed throughout this book. Yet they (we) fail to confront the *central* issue, the issue of an activist government,[42] because in the current climate it is anathema. However, it is precisely as Theodore Roosevelt said:

> There was a time when the limitation of governmen-
> tal power meant increasing liberty for the people. In
> the present day, the limitation of governmental
> power, of governmental action, means the enslave-
> ment of the people by the great corporations.[43]

In the face of a global economy and rapid technological development, in the face of the pathologies that have been brought by a blind and dogmatic *laissez-faire* ideology in the United States, we need a mixed economy, with countervailing institutions (including carefully thought-out regulatory instruments) and a vigorous public sector. We need a strong and vigilant government, answerable to us all. We shall be lost without it.

These are at the center of reform. Also, every citizen needs a determination to use the sharp edge of cynicism, which has now been bred in most of us, to pare away sound bites and self-interest and get at the heart of issues—of some issues or even one or two issues. Citizens need a critical reexamination of the ethical basis of their occupation or profession—medicine, social science, education, the ministry, social service, law and journalism in particular. And the nation needs from citizens an activist stance, whether simply in expressing themselves or in political or corporate life, depending on where they are and the style with which they address life and their companions.

A small book called *Failed Revolutions* examines a number of attempts at legal reform; the name of the book announces the authors' conclusion. In addressing the question of what is needed for reform, the books adds this:

> An individual who understands the ways near-uni-
> versal forces resist change is better armored against
> self-blame. He or she realizes that failure is not al-
> ways the result of lack of skill or nerve, that the real
> question is often not, Why go on? but, Why quit?[44]

Why, indeed! In the heart and the mind, a struggle for decency and social justice—win or lose—feels far better than resignation or opting out. And, in accordance with the theory of punctuated equilibrium, one understands that reform may dawn unexpectedly. The greedy have overreached by far: The strains and stresses that people experience are widely felt, if not observed by those who may have much to lose. The pressure for change must be accumulating just as it did, unobserved, for so many years before it raised up the civil rights movement and brought down the Berlin Wall. The determined efforts of reformers and humanitarians will certainly bring the day of change—of punctuation—closer.

ॐ

NOTES

1. Henry Adams, "A Dynamic Theory of History," in *The Education of Henry Adams*, Houghton Mifflin, Boston, 1918, p. 483. Or, ". . . Henry has demonstrated certain facts. The first great fact is that science is sunk in such chaos that . . . it is impossible to show that the world itself, or man as a portion of the world, has evolved in obedience to any single power which might be called a unified creator. His tendency is always to suggest complexity as a motor. Therefore, democracy must partake of the complexity of its infinitely complex creator and ultimately end in chaos." "Introductory Note," by Brooks Adams, in *Henry Adams: The Degradation of the Democratic Dogma*, P. Smith, publisher, 1949, p. viii.

2. Alvin L. Schorr, "The Myths that Help Us Ignore Poverty," *Washington Post*, Outlook Section, 18 December 1977.

3. William Graebner, *A History of Retirement: The Meaning and Function of an American Institution, 1885–1978*, Yale University Press, New Haven, Connecticut, 1980.

4. David M. Gordon, *Fat and Mean: The Corporate Squeeze of Working Americans and the Myth of Managerial Downsizing*, Free Press, New York, 1996.

5. Estimate by Secretary of Labor Robert B. Reich, *New York Times*, 11 September 1993.

6. Louis Uchitelle, "Despite Drop, Rate of Layoffs Remains High," *New York Times*, 23 August 1996.

7. Louis Uchitelle and N. R. Kleinfeld, "On the Battlefields of Business, Millions of Casualties," *New York Times*, 3 March 1996.

8. Robert Kuttner, *The End of Laissez-Faire, National Purpose and the Global Economy After the Cold War*, Alfred A. Knopf, New York, 1991.

9. W. B. Yeats, "The Second Coming," from *Michael Robartes and the Dancer* (1921), in *The Collected Poems of W. B. Yeats*, Macmillan, New York, 1950, p. 184.

10. John Donne, "The First Anniversary, An Anatomy of the World" (1611), in C. A. Patrides, ed., *John Donne, The Complete Poems*, Dent, Everyman's Library, London, 1985.

11. Emile Durkheim, in *Suicide*, G. Simpson, ed., Routledge and Kegan Paul, London, 1952.

12. George Steiner, "The Dissent from Reason—Contemporary Intellectual Currents in the Western World," The B'nai B'rith Jerusalem Address, 1986. Processed.

13. Marie Jahoda, *Employment and Unemployment*, Cambridge University Press, Cambridge, U.K., 1982, p. 39.

14. M. Harvey Brenner, *Estimating the Effects of Economic Change on National Health and Social Well-Being*, A Study for the U.S. Congress, Joint Economic Committee, U.S. Government Printing Office, Washington, D.C., 1984.

15. Mary Merva and Richard Fowles, *Effects of Diminished Opportunities on Social Stress: Heart Attacks, Strokes, and Crime*, Economic Policy Institute, Washington, D.C., 1996.

16. W. G. Runciman, *Relative Deprivation and Social Justice*, Routledge and Kegan Paul, London, 1966.

17. Quoted in the *Washington Post*, 29 November 1996, editorial page.

18. Center on Budget and Policy Priorities, *Poverty and Income Trends: 1994*, March 1996. "Average Family Income by Quintiles," table, p. 59. Part of a jump in income for the top quintile between 1992 and 1993 is attributed to a change in census methodology. However, it appears that without a change in methodology the 1994 ratio would still have worked out to 11 to 1 or close to it.

19. The United Nations Development Program publishes somewhat different ratios for the United States and other countries, primarily because it averages together the ratios for the years since 1981, thus tending to minimize the effect of recent sharp changes. For 1981–93, it shows a U.S. ratio of 8.9, with higher ratios only for Australia and the United Kingdom (both 9.6) and the Russian Federation (11.4). *Human Development Report 1996*, Oxford University Press, New York, 1996.

20. Dr. Reva Gurstein, chair, Jacques Labelle, Dr. Stuart McLeod, Dr. Fraser Mustard, Dr. Robert Spasoff, Joan Watson, *Nurturing Health—A Framework on the Determinants of Health,* The Premier's Council on Health Strategy, Province of Ontario, Toronto, 1990. This document contains the briefest of summaries of the research evidence on this point. See also Kennedy et al. and Kaplan et al. in the *British Medical Journal,* April 1996, cited in the *PNHP Newsletter,* July 1996.

21. James Q. Wilson, "The Rediscovery of Character: Private Virtue and Public Policy," *The Public Interest,* Fall 1985, p. 3, quoted in Michael J. Sandel, *Democracy's Discontent: America in Search of Public Policy,* The Belknap Press of Harvard University Press, Cambridge, Massachusetts, 1996.

22. Sandel, ibid, p. 326.

23. Senator Joseph McCarthy, who conducted the infamous U.S. Senate hearings about communism in the government in the 1950s, devoted his very first hearing to investigating the administration of public assistance.

24. Sandel, op. cit.

25. Kristin Luker, *Dubious Conceptions: The Politics of Teen Age Pregnancy,* Harvard University Press, Cambridge, Massachusetts, 1996.

26. James A. Morone, "The Corrosive Politics of Virtue," *The American Prospect,* May-June 1996.

27. Stanley K. Henshaw and Jennifer Van Vort, "Abortion Services in the United States, 1991 and 1992," *Family Planning Perspectives,* 26, 1994.

28. Lisa Kaesar, Rachel Benson Gold and Cory L. Richards, *Title X at 25,* The Alan Guttmacher Institute, CITY?, 1996.

29. William Ruefle and Kenneth Mike Reynolds, "Curfews and Delinquency in Major American Cities," *Crime and Delinquency,* July 1995.

30. W. Wesley Johnson, "Transcarceration and Social Control Policy: The 1980s and Beyond," *Crime and Delinquency,* January 1996, p. 114.

31. Nina Bernstein, "New, Tougher Policies Raise Issues of Fairness to Women," *New York Times,* 20 August 1996. Reversing a lower court's sentence of a woman (who had two young children and an infant she was breast feeding) to a residential treatment center (where her children could stay with her) and to a correctional halfway house, the District of Columbia Appeals Court wrote that: "The unfortunate fact is that some mothers are criminals and, like it or not, incarceration is our criminal justice system's principal method of punishment. A term in jail will always separate a mother from her children."

32. Apropos is a line in a poem by Jacques Prévert, *Selections from Paroles,*

Penguin Modern European Poets, p. 110: "It is not necessary to let the intellectuals play with the matches." For a painstaking examination of "labeling" and the role of scholars, see Herbert J. Gans, *The War Against the Poor*, Basic Books, New York, 1995.

33. For a careful description of these developments, see Gary Mucchiaroni, *Reversals of Fortune, Public Policy and Private Interests*, The Brookings Institution, Washington, D.C., 1995.

34. Congressman Peter A. Fazio, quoted in "TCI Plan to Cut Lifetime Angers Women's Groups," *New York Times*, 14 September 1996.

35. "Laws Won't Let H.M.O.s Tell Doctors What to Say," *New York Times*, 17 September 1996, p. A9.

36. Roger D. Colton, "The Need for Regulation in a Competitive Electric Utility Industry," Fisher, Sheehan & Colton, Belmont, Massachusetts, pp. 3, 4. Processed.

37. Richard L. Grossman and Ward Morehouse, "Minorities, the Poor & Ending Corporate Rule," *Poverty and Race*, 4, no. 5, September/October 1995, p. 3.

38. Howard Schweber, "The Duties of the Postmodern Corporation," Odyssey Forum, P.O. Box 1223, McLean, Virginia. Processed.

39. Grossman and Morehouse, op. cit., pp. 3, 4.

40. Eileen Appelbaum, Peter Berg and Dean Baker, "The Economic Case for Corporate Responsibility to Workers," Issue Brief #111, Economic Policy Institute, Washington, D.C., 3 April 1996, p. 4.

41. Cited in Jeff Faux, *The Party's Not Over*, Basic Books, New York, 1996.

42. More or less as I write, however, these arguments for an activist government appear: Robert Kuttner, *Everything for Sale*, Twentieth Century Fund/Alfred A. Knopf, New York, 1997; William Greider, *One World, Ready or Not*, Simon & Schuster, New York, 1997; George Soros, "The Capitalist Threat," *The Atlantic Monthly*, February 1997; and Paul Krugman, "We Are Not the World," *New York Times*, 13 February 1997, op-ed page.

43. Quoted in Walter Russell Mead, "Newt's Real Target: The Other Roosevelt," *New York Times Magazine*, 15 October 1995, p. 59. See also Sandel, op. cit., p. 346.

44. Richard Delgado and Jean Stefanic, *Failed Revolutions*, Westview Press, Boulder, Colorado, 1994.

Index

ORDER FORM

Please photocopy this page to order additional copies of *Passion and Policy.*

Yes, please send me:

QUANTITY

_____ *Passion and Policy* by Alvin L. Schorr. **$29.95 hardcover.** Plus $4.50 shipping and handling for one copy, $1.25 more for each additional copy. Ohio residents add 5.75% state sales tax to the retail cost of the books.

_____ *Passion and Policy* by Alvin L. Schorr. **$19.95 softcover.** Plus $3.50 shipping and handling for one copy, $1 more for each additional copy. Ohio residents add 5.75% state sales tax to the retail cost of the books.

For special rates for bulk orders, contact David Press, an imprint of Octavia Press, at the address below.

☐ Check made payable to Octavia Press enclosed

Name _____

Street address _____
(No P.O. Box numbers, please; we ship UPS.)

City _____

Daytime phone no. _____

☐ Please send a gift copy of *Passion and Policy* to:

Name _____

Street address _____
(No P.O. Box numbers, please; we ship UPS.)

City _____

Gift message to read: _____

_____

Mail payment and order form to:

Octavia Press
12127 Sperry Road
Chesterland, OH 44026

(440) 729-3252